STANDING TOGETHER

THE INSPIRATIONAL STORY *of a*
WOUNDED WARRIOR *and* ENDURING LOVE

Carlos R. Evans *and* Rosemarie Evans
with Cecil Murphey

Standing Together: The Inspirational Story of a Wounded Warrior and Enduring Love
© 2019 Carlos R. Evans and Rosemarie Evans

Published by Kregel Publications, a division of Kregel Inc., 2450 Oak Industrial Dr. NE, Grand Rapids, MI 49505.

This work of creative nonfiction is told from the authors' perspectives and recalled to the best of their memories.

This is one couple's story. The path to recovery presented in this book is not intended as a guide to diagnose or treat medical or psychological problems. If medical, psychological, or other expert assistance is required, the reader should seek the services of a health-care provider or certified counselor.

All photographs have been provided by Carlos R. Evans and permission for use of photographs is the responsibility of the author.

Scripture quotations are from the Holy Bible, New International Version®, NIV®. Copyright © 1973, 1978, 1984, 2011 by Biblica, Inc.™ Used by permission of Zondervan. All rights reserved worldwide. www .zondervan.com. The "NIV" and "New International Version" are trademarks registered in the United States Patent and Trademark Office by Biblica, Inc.™

ISBN 978-0-8254-4497-5, print
ISBN 978-0-8254-7454-5, epub

Printed in the United States of America
19 20 21 22 23 24 25 26 27 28 / 5 4 3 2 1

"This is a tremendous story of resilience and hope. Carlos and Rosemarie Evans tell a powerful personal account of overcoming trauma and tragedy. In so doing, they give hope to all who have experienced and are experiencing the wounds of war."

—TIMOTHY J. DEMY, ThD, PhD, professor of
military ethics, US Naval War College,
and retired chaplain, US Navy

"Carlos and Rosemarie will bring you to tears—and cheers—with their frank story of hardship—and victory—after major trauma. Their vivid narrative of tough times, tough love, and God's grace shows the way through both terrible circumstances and struggles of the soul. They don't give you a feel-good formula or how-to tale. They do share how they beat the odds against survival and recovery by leaning on God and all the good people in their lives. You don't have to love God or love marines to be enriched here, but you cannot read their story without coming to love Carlos and Rosemarie and being grateful for this time spent with them. You'll learn from them that with Christ all things are possible!"

—MARK A. JUMPER, PhD, director of Chaplaincy and
Military Affairs and assistant professor,
Regent University School of Divinity

For our beloved daughters,
Nairoby and Genesis

Now I have one hand,
and I'm touching more people than when I had two.
I don't have feet,
but I'm leaving more footprints than when I had two.

—Carlos Evans

Contents

1

The Phone Call

Rosemarie

Even though he couldn't call often, the phone call on Saturday, May 15, 2010, from Carlos was different from any of the others. Afterward, I couldn't stop crying.

He was on his fourth deployment, this time in Afghanistan. The previous three deployments had been in Iraq. Because of the time difference—they were nine and a half hours ahead of us in Fajardo, Puerto Rico—I was never surprised when he called at strange hours. I was so glad to hear from him, I didn't care if it was the middle of the night. Each call meant he was safe, and I was relieved.

I had flown to Puerto Rico, and that Saturday I had gone out of town for my uncle's wedding. Now, back at my mother's, I was putting both daughters to bed. My cell rang. Caller ID showed me it was a strange number, such as 1111111111, so I knew it was Carlos.

"Hey, baby, how are you?" I asked.

"I'm fine."

His voice sounded flat, unlike him. I was excited to hear from him, yet his tone upset me. "Baby, are you okay?"

"Everything here is different than before."

That was an odd thing for him to say and nothing like the usual upbeat Carlos. After a pause, he said, "You know I love you, don't you? You know that you and my daughters are the most important part of my life."

"Yes," I said, "and you're the most important person in my life."

What's wrong? What isn't he telling me?

"Everything is different here, but I'm thinking about you all the time." Then he repeated, "You're the most important person in my life."

The phone went dead.

Why did he hang up? What's happened to him? Why was he talking that way? Was he saying goodbye to me? Is he in the hospital? Has he been badly wounded?

My tears flowed. I couldn't call him back because I didn't know his number. All night long I couldn't stop crying. I'd fall asleep for a few minutes and wake up sobbing. *No, dear Lord, don't . . . don't let him die.*

All the next day I waited for my cell to ring, but no calls came from Carlos. I didn't cry as much, but I fretted. I couldn't focus clearly on things I had to do because I kept hearing that sad tone in his voice. Then I would cry out to God to take care of him. For a short time I'd feel at peace, but minutes later I'd worry about him again.

Before going out of town, I had made a number of things to mail to Carlos, such as a photo blanket collage and a photo dog tag with our wedding picture, and I put photographs of the girls and me in an album. Our anniversary was a month away, and I wanted him to have those things because he was away from us. Father's Day was also in June, and I wanted it to be a special occasion for him and a reminder of how much we loved and missed him.

After the phone call, I didn't know if I should mail the package or not. Finally I pushed away my negative thoughts about Carlos. If he had been badly injured or worse, the Marine Corps would have notified me. No notification must mean he was all right.

I kept repeating those words to myself. Slowly I calmed down and was able to focus on making him happy. Once Carlos receives the package, I told myself several times, he'll be reminded that we love him, and we didn't forget him while he was gone.

I thought of Carlos's mother, Virginia Evans, who also lived in Fajardo, Puerto Rico. I had worked hard on the blanket and decided to show her everything I was going to send him. I drove to her house that day on my way to the post office.

Virginia smiled as she examined the contents. "Oh, this is all so pretty." She picked up the blanket and the photographs one by one and assured me that her son would like everything.

After I expressed my concern over the telephone call, she hugged me and assured me that Carlos was fine and reminded me, "He's in God's hands."

"I know." Being with Virginia often eased my concern about Carlos's safety.

I sealed the package and drove to the post office. Before I got there, my cell rang. It was a local number that I didn't recognize. "Hello," I said.

"Is your name Rosemarie Evans?" a man asked.

"Yes, it's me."

He identified himself as being with the Marine Corps. After that I don't remember anything else until he added. "We're in front of your mother-in-law's house. We need you to come back immediately."

They knew how to reach me because earlier that morning

I had received a call from the Family Support Program in Camp Lejeune at Jacksonville, North Carolina. The caller asked me how I was doing and where I was staying. I gave him the address of my mother-in-law.

> More than once my husband had said,
> "If you see marines in front of the house,
> they're going to tell you bad news."

"What's wrong?" My voice was shaking, but I couldn't stop it.

"We're waiting for you," he said. "We'll explain when you get here."

"No! No!" I yelled before I hung up. They had terrible news to tell me. *Carlos is dead. That's why he called yesterday. He was dying.*

More than once my husband had said, "If you see marines in front of the house, they're going to tell you bad news."

As I drove back, I thought of what I'd seen in movies when two military officers knocked on the door. Only the year before, Carlos and I had watched the film *Taking Chance*, in which the body of Lance Corporal Chance Phelps, an Iraq war casualty, is escorted home by Marine Colonel Michael Strobl (played by Kevin Bacon).

Carlos is dead. I was crying so hard that several times I had to brush away tears so I could see well enough to drive. I kept screaming, "No! No! Not Carlos!"

When I reached Virginia's house, three marines stood next to a government car in front. I parked my car, ignored them, and rushed up to the house. It sounds silly now, but it was as if I didn't have to talk to them in order to know my Carlos was gone.

I started knocking on the door and yelling, "Virginia!"

She opened the door, shocked at seeing me. "Why have you come back so fast? Why are you crying?"

"Virginia, they're here! They're here!"

Virginia shook her head, confused. "Who's here?"

I turned and pointed to the marines in dress uniform who were walking up the driveway.

Then she knew.

Virginia grabbed me, and we both cried uncontrollably for several seconds. The three men stood in front of us, saying nothing.

As soon as we calmed down a little, one of them said, "May we come inside?"

Virginia nodded and opened the door for them.

Once inside, one of them looked straight at me before he said, "Mrs. Evans, we are here because we have to notify you that your husband was on foot patrol. He stepped on a bomb, on an IED—"*

"Is he—is he dead?"

"He lost both legs instantly, and we cannot assure you whether he is still alive."

I was so emotionally overwrought that I heard only "lost both legs."

"Is my son still alive?" Virginia asked.

"We do not know," the man said softly. "He was badly hurt, and doctors have been trying to assess his wounds."

"We came to prepare you," said one of them, who identified

---

* An IED, or improvised explosive device, is a bomb with a detonating mechanism, made in an unconventional way. IEDs are commonly used as roadside bombs.

himself as a chaplain. "Because of the time difference, we need you to get prepared for the worst—for everything."

I started crying again, and this time I stopped thinking about myself or missing him but thought instead of how much Carlos must be hurting. I'm a nurse and had recently updated my certificate and received my license for prehospital trauma life support. The course had focused on accidents outside the hospital and included studies on people who had lost arms and legs after blasts such as explosions or bombs. I knew too much to listen objectively.

My whole system went numb. My tears continued to flow, but I couldn't think or say anything as I stared at them.

Then the chaplain began to pray and pulled me back to reality. His voice sounded like someone speaking with authority and compassion.

One man had given me the bad news, and now the second was asking God to give me the strength to bear it, no matter what happened. His powerful words calmed me, and I was able to stop crying.

As soon as the marines left, I called my dad and other family members. All of us are Puerto Rican and part of a closely knit family. I didn't trust myself to drive to my house, so I asked Dad to come over to take me to his home. My mother was taking care of my two daughters.

When we reached my parents' house, Mom saw my face and asked, "What happened to you?"

"Carlos was injured and . . ." I broke down, and between convulsive sobs, I told her everything.

Mom held me and started praying. Afterward she said, "I'll take care of the girls. You take care of yourself."

Within an hour, the word had spread among our family and close friends, and the house filled with relatives and church members. Many were kneeling or standing as they prayed. I looked around, grateful to God that we had a wonderful support system. As more family and friends arrived, I began to feel better.

With God's help and the support of my friends, I can survive this.

I reminded myself, Carlos is still alive. He may not have legs, but he'll still be Carlos. He's the only man I have ever loved. Each time tears came, someone seemed to grab me and pray for me.

"Don't believe Carlos will die," more than one person said. "Trust God, and we're all believing for the Lord to spare him."

Others promised they would come to see me every day to pray with me and to let me know they were with me in my pain.

The first time I heard those words, I didn't want to inconvenience them. "You don't have to come. You can call me—"

"No! I want to be here—to see you face-to-face," one friend said. "I can't do that by phone."

Then everyone was gone. I waited and prayed. Time seemed to drag by, and I frequently checked my phone to make sure the sound was on and that it was fully charged.

When I was finally alone, with my two daughters asleep, God's peace came over me and I slept.

The next day, a marine officer called and said matter-of-factly, "We can say nothing by phone. Please wait at the Diaz home for us to inform you of the circumstances." They didn't say when they would come.

I clung to the fact that he used the word *circumstances* instead of saying Carlos had been killed. I was filled with anxiety, wanting to know, and many times gave way to tears. Finally, about five o'clock, they arrived. By that time, once again the house had filled up with family members and friends.

"Is he—is he alive?" Carlos's mother asked.

"Yes, as far as we know," one of them said.

"Everything remains the same," the marine liaison said. "Your husband is still at the military hospital, Landstuhl Regional Medical Center in Germany."

They had nothing more to tell me and left.

True to their word, those friends and relatives who promised to visit me each day came to see me. Their prayers and encouragement comforted me, but I still had no real answers. Carlos was alive, but . . .

"No! He's alive!" I shouted. "He is alive." I cried off and on through the night. I was such a mess that I couldn't take care of Nairoby, who was three years old, and Genesis, who was barely at the crawling stage. I finally called my mother, and she took care of our two children. That made me feel guilty, but I wasn't emotionally able to give them what they needed. I couldn't eat, and I slept little. I felt deep pain in my heart that wouldn't let go.

The next day, about the same time, the same marines came. When I saw their faces, I started to cry again.

Then the first marine smiled.

That's when I knew my husband was still alive.

2

The Left Handprint

Carlos

After six years in the Marine Corps, I was on my fourth deployment as a squad leader in Afghanistan. Most of the time we did foot patrols. On May 15, 2010, however, we drove to our next mission to set up a security post, and this time I was the squad leader of a vehicle patrol. As we did each day, we were driving a Humvee around the area, searching for unsuspected activity and IEDs. Technically the vehicle was called a High Mobility Multipurpose Wheeled Vehicle (HMMWV), a four-wheel drive military light truck. We frequently faced combat and never knew when we'd be engaged, so we drove slowly and carefully.

Without warning, my body was thrown forward. An explosive noise filled my ears. We had driven over an IED.

Everything went black.

For a few seconds I must have been unconscious, and then I revived. I was relieved that I felt no pain. My driver and the gunner were both unconscious, and when they came to, they were in shock. I called every man by name, and each said, "Okay," or "Fine."

Once certain that everyone was all right, I got out of the vehicle. I was amazed that we had run over an IED and none of us sustained injuries. I called for support—we needed to get transport back to base because our vehicle had been too badly damaged to drive.

I knew of too many incidents of Humvees hitting IEDs in which one or more of those inside the vehicle died or were badly wounded. Right then, I stopped and prayed silently. "Oh God, I could have lost my life. Thank you, thank you for taking care of all of us."

I was grateful to be alive, and I tried to keep my mind free of what might have been. After we returned to base camp, I kept thinking that I might not have returned. That explosion was the closest I had come to physical injury. I turned my thoughts to Rosemarie and how grateful I was to be alive and to have such a godly wife.

I needed someone to talk to, and I missed my wife. I was alive, grateful, and rejoicing, and I yearned to hear her voice. I don't recall ever being more emotional or feeling so alone and in need of my family.

I called Rosemarie. I didn't tell her about the narrow escape with the IED explosion. "It doesn't matter what happens to me here, I want you to always know how much I love you."

Those were my last words because the battery on my satellite phone died without warning. While I charged it, I decided to write her a letter telling her how much I loved her and missed her.

I stopped and stared at the wedding ring on my left hand. That was a powerful moment for me because the ring symbolized my devotion and commitment. *I'll always be here for you, Rosemarie.*

I'm not sure why, but I decided to make a photocopy of my left hand, where I normally wore my wedding ring. On the corner of the photo, I wrote, "This is so you know when

I'm not here you can look at my hand, you can look at my wedding ring and know how much I love you, that I'm always going to be here for you."

As I stared at the photocopy, I carefully sketched my wife and two kids on my hand. It was my way to say, "It doesn't matter what happens, we're always going to be together, and I love you."

I finished the letter, enclosed the photocopy, and put the envelope in the outgoing mail.

During that deployment and the three previous ones, until the day of the explosion, I don't think I ever considered that anything was going to happen to me. I personally knew others who had died and some who were badly wounded, but as a Christian, I figured God was with me and would protect me from every kind of harm.

On my various furloughs, I said to friends and family members, "I'm not going to die in Iraq or Afghanistan. God has a bigger purpose for my life."

The day after I wrote the letter to Rosemarie, our squad went out on foot patrol. We were in firefights almost every day, so there was heavy combat while we were there, but none close to us. Besides my squad, we also had plenty of support with us. As we went out, I prayed as I usually did before going on foot patrol, asking God to protect us and bring us all back safely. As we left base, I felt confident. I felt very good.

That morning I led eighteen men on foot patrol. We found two IEDs, which Staff Sergeant David Lyon deactivated.

Lyon was a specialist in explosive ordinance detection (EOD) and was excellent at locating and deactivating IEDs before we walked on them or our vehicles drove over them. We also had a trained dog with us who was good at sniffing out IEDs. Lyon and the others had gotten good at mastering their equipment. After they found the first two bombs, all of us in the squad seemed more confident.

After a time, it seemed we were on safe ground, so the EOD people left us and went with another squad in a different direction. I was all right with their leaving, but I called out to Lyon, "I'm probably going to call you back because I know we're going to find more IEDs."

A few minutes later, we went into a deserted house and found several IEDs, so I called David Lyon, who had also become a good friend. "I told you I would probably call you back. We've located more IEDs. You've got to deactivate them."

Lyon came and did his work. While he was doing that, I got on the radio with my commanding officer (CO). As I stood outside the house, I spotted something suspicious in the area and told him. "Before we return to base, we'll check it out," Lyon said.

We were in a country of rock and sand, and the temperature was high. The equipment we carried probably weighed fifty pounds. By then we were worn out from the heat, the walking, and our intense concentration on the ground.

A dog handler was on my right side and a corpsman on my left. I needed to see where my squad members were positioned before we started back. I stood, then walked about eight steps up a small incline to see everyone.

Those eight steps were the last ones I ever took on my own two legs.

The area was supposed to have been cleared. As I took the next step, a loud booming sound filled the air—an explosion that seemed far away. I wondered what it was because I was still alive. I didn't know it, but I had stepped on an IED. A beeping sound filled my left ear.

I called, "Doc! Doc!" I had been knocked down and I wanted to be sure no one was hurt.

I was on the ground looking up, and three of my team members surrounded me. The corpsman bent over me. The noise of the detonation had temporarily deafened me. I could see his lips moving, but I couldn't hear any words. From the expression on his face, I knew someone had been hurt.

Someone, probably the corpsman, shouted, and I barely heard the words, "You're going to be all right! Everything is going to be all right!"

I must have stared in confusion. "Hey, how's everybody? What's going on? What happened?"

"Evans, you're going to be all right! You're going to be all right."

By now I was able to hear. "Why do you keep saying that? What happened?"

I always assumed that if something went wrong, I would be the one taking care of others, helping them and talking to them. I was their leader. *This isn't right. I'm not supposed to be hurt. God wouldn't let this happen to me.*

A deep tiredness came over me; I could feel myself fading. That's when I realized I must be losing blood—a lot of blood. It was getting harder and harder to stay awake, and all I wanted to do was sleep. I closed my eyes.

"Get up! Get up!" one of my buddies yelled out. He or someone else slapped my face a couple of times, which momentarily revived me. "Evans, you're going to be all right!"

The realization hit me. *I'm dying. I'm not going to make it.* I tried to cry out—whether I actually did or only wanted to, I don't know: "I can't be dying. I can't die. I'm not supposed to die here in Afghanistan. I told my wife I was coming back in six months. She's waiting for me back home, and I have a project to complete with my daughter. We started painting the playground around our new house. I promised to come back and finish painting it with her."

*God, you can't let me die now. You have a
bigger purpose in my life. This can't be the end.*

I can't die. I can't die. Too many things in life I haven't done yet.

But I'm dying.

Rosemarie, I'm sorry. I should have been more available to you. I should have told you more often that I loved you and been there more with our daughters.

"Tell her—tell Rosemarie how much I love her." One of the men told me I said that out loud.

God, you can't let me die now. You have a bigger purpose in my life. This can't be the end.

When I was a kid, my great-grandmother used to say to me, "God has a purpose for you, Carlos. A great purpose." As I lay dying I smiled, thinking of the many times she said, "You're going to be a pastor and tell people about Jesus Christ."

She spoke that way to me because, as the youngest of four, I kept screaming and yelling. Now once again I was yelling. I couldn't believe what was happening to me. I should have ended the mission and gone back to the base with the whole platoon. Instead, in a kind of crazy, semiconscious state, I was calling out orders of what I should have done.

Finally I stopped yelling and went silent. In that moment, I surrendered myself to God. "If this is your time for me, here I am. Everything I believed in—your great purpose for me—it wasn't true, was it? You've left me and I'm going to die here." Doubts filled my mind, and yet at the same time I knew I was ready to go.

Then the shock wore off.

And like a bolt of lightning, the pain hit.

3

Alive!

Agony, sudden and overpowering. I was already lying on the ground. The desert and the blazing sun no longer felt hot. My corpsman later told me that he could see I was in acute pain, and he had trouble stopping the bleeding. "I had to put nine tourniquets on your body," he said. "I put four on your right leg, four on your left, and one on your arm."

The worst source of bleeding was my right leg. The corpsman pressed his thumb on it. "I put my thumb there," he said, "to keep you alive."

I couldn't see what was happening. My whole body was suddenly on fire, and there wasn't any place I didn't hurt. Never in my entire life had I ever experienced such trauma. They tell me I started yelling. "I can't take any more! Oh God, if I had only turned and gone back, this wouldn't have happened!" I was angry, and I think I was scared.

"God, let me die! Let me die! I can't deal with this!" I forgot about God's purpose; I forgot about my family; I forgot about everything because I was going through so much agony.

Corporal Jessy Maynard was in front of me, and while the corpsman worked, Maynard kept yelling, "Sergeant Evans! You're not going to die! Not today! You're going to go home! You're going to get out of this stinking desert!"

He was holding my right hand and kept yelling. I tried to smile and believe his words.

"You're going to get out of this place. You're going to go home and you're going to eat some ice cream! You know, ice cream is heaven in the desert. You're going to go home! You're going to eat ice cream! A lot of ice cream."

I could see his face and kept thinking, Leave me alone! I'm dying. Let me die in peace.

"What's your wife's name?" Maynard asked. I was staring at him, and all I wanted to do was sleep. He was keeping me awake with his questions.

"Hey, what's your wife's name? What's your wife's name?"

"Rosemarie."

"What are your girls' names?" All the men knew I had two daughters. And we shared pictures, especially those of us who were married.

Why is he asking that? He knows.

"Sergeant Evans, what are the names of your daughters?"

"Genesis . . . and . . . Nairoby . . ."

"Talk to me about your family. Where did you meet Rosemarie?" He kept asking me, and with great effort I answered. When I didn't, he'd stick his face only inches from mine and yell until I responded.

As much as I was positive I was dying, Maynard's questions gave me strength to fight.

"You want to see them again! You do, don't you?"

"Yes . . ."

"What are you going to do with them?"

". . . Paint . . . playground . . ."

As I kept answering, for the first time I knew I couldn't die. *I won't die!* I could hear myself yelling—or maybe it only felt like yelling—"Lord, forgive me for failing you in so many ways. Give me the strength to go home and see my family. I know they're waiting for me. They're waiting . . ."

Thinking of my family was the last thing I remember.

From the others, I learned that they got me back to camp, and I was medevacked by helicopter. There was another big explosion as the helicopter took off. I didn't know what happened in that second blast because I was too much out of it. Later I would learn about the effects of that blast.

They took me to the military hospital at Bagram, Afghanistan. The crew of the helicopter and the medevac team kept me alive. Most of them were sure I wouldn't make it, but they still refused to give up on me.

I survived. For that, I thank God and my fellow marines.

Rosemarie

Once those marines let me know that Carlos was still alive, they came every day to visit. They gave me whatever updates they could, which mostly were to reassure me that doctors were doing everything possible for him.

"Your husband has been sent from Bagram Air Force Base in Afghanistan," the marine liaison told me, "to the Landstuhl Regional Medical Center in Germany."

I asked questions, but again, the message was the same: "He is alive. We can tell you nothing more about his condition." He handed me a piece of paper. "Here's a telephone number you can call. We understand he's in ICU, but you can talk to his nurse."

I don't know if I hugged them or not, but I cried. I was relieved that Carlos was alive—but how much alive, I didn't know. At the moment, that part didn't matter.

Thank you, Lord, for sparing him. Thank you that he's alive.

Before their car pulled out of the driveway, I dialed the number. As expected, a nurse answered. I told her who I was and said, "The marine liaison gave me this number . . ."

She started to explain his injuries in simple terms, and I stopped her. "I'm a nurse. Tell me, how bad is he? What are you doing for him?"

"Right now, he's connected to a ventilator," she said, which meant they had inserted a tube in his trachea with anesthesia. "We had to amputate his left hand because it was too badly damaged."

By then I was crying, and the nurse hesitated.

"Please tell me. I am his wife, and I'm saddened, but I want to know everything." She told me that he had lost both legs before he arrived in Germany, and they were still giving him tests. "He's sedated and he has a Bogota bag."*

I asked more questions, but she said, "I'm sorry, but it will be a day or two before we can tell you anything more."

> "God, I don't care if he doesn't have legs.
> I don't care if he doesn't have a left hand.
> I want him to come back to us alive."

I thanked her, relieved that Carlos was alive. Knowing that fact lifted my spirits. After I hung up, however, I felt numb for several minutes. He would have no legs, and now they had removed his left hand. Parts of him were being taken away.

What if they want to take more?

Fresh tears came, but they were different this time. Less

---

* A Bogota bag is a sterile plastic bag used for closure of wounds.

painful. *Carlos is alive.* I had to keep reminding myself that he was alive and in a hospital in Germany. Knowing that strengthened me.

"God, I don't care if he doesn't have legs. I don't care if he doesn't have a left hand. I want him to come back to us alive."

I thought about Carlos when he was home with me here in North Carolina. So many times I had been too busy cleaning or taking care of the girls and had neglected him. Had I failed him as his wife? Was God punishing me for that?

Those weren't healthy thoughts, but I knew I hadn't said "I love you" often enough to Carlos. Too many times I had taken our wonderful relationship for granted. "God, I promise you I won't let that happen again. I'll tell him and show him how much I love him. Please bring him back. I don't care how he comes back; just bring him home alive."

At noon on May 21, a marine called and asked, "Do you have your luggage ready? Tell your in-laws that we're making arrangements to fly you and them to Bethesda . . ."

He spoke so matter-of-factly I could hardly absorb it all, so he repeated everything and added, "Today your husband is being transferred to Bethesda Hospital in Washington, DC. You will be able to visit him tomorrow."†

I can see him tomorrow! I can see him tomorrow!

Knowing that pushed away my worries and concerns. We would be together soon. And once we were together, we could handle anything.

I believed that, but the following months tested my faith in God and in our relationship.

---

† In 2010, Walter Reed and Bethesda were two different places. Bethesda was the hospital for marines and navy; Walter Reed was the army hospital. Carlos had his surgeries at Bethesda and did his physical therapy at Walter Reed.

4

Alive . . . But

Carlos's parents and I arrived at Bethesda Naval Hospital before midnight on May 21, 2010. Someone escorted us to the correct ward, and a nurse was waiting for us. She told us about Carlos's condition and collected family information from me.

"Right now, doctors are doing a CT scan. When he was transferred, he wasn't responding well."

Because I'm a nurse, my immediate thought was, What if he has brain damage? I tried to thrust that out of my mind, but I couldn't. Regardless, he was the man I loved—the man God sent into my life—and we would still be together.

After his CT scan, the nurse said, "He's sleeping, but you can see him." They told me Carlos was on the third floor in the intensive care unit at Walter Reed.

If I hadn't been a nurse, I probably would have been shocked to see that he was connected to a ventilator, and they had put on three wound VACs.* I studied the monitor, which showed me that his vital signs were good. I felt relieved.

"Carlos. Carlos."

Slowly he opened his brown eyes, and they flickered in

---

* VACs, or vacuum-assisted closures, decrease the amount of time needed to heal and greatly reduce the risk of infection.

recognition and then shock—I think because he didn't know how I had gotten to him. Tears rolled down his cheeks.

I smiled. I was happy that he recognized me. *He knows me! He knows me!* Relief filled my soul and I thought, He'll be all right. We can make it together.

Because of the tubes, Carlos couldn't talk, but he began pointing toward his legs. I didn't realize that he didn't know they were gone, but I knew about amputation and phantom pain.

"It's all right, baby, lie still." I leaned over and kissed his forehead. "I love you and the girls love you." I talked softly to him, and he closed his eyes and went back to sleep.

We left the room, and as soon as we closed the door, I said to Carlos's parents, Virginia and Rafael, "He recognized me. He knows who we are!"

Carlos

I recall nothing until the seventh day after my accident. I opened my eyes, and Rosemarie was sitting beside my bed, staring at me. I blinked several times, wanting to be sure that what I saw was real.

Then I smiled. I tried to laugh and yell, but I couldn't because my throat hurt so badly. But inside I was yelling, God! I'm alive! I'm alive!

I'm alive! God answered my prayer. That's how I remember it. Rosemarie told me I looked up, saw her, and started crying. I was intubated, and I kept trying to say, "My throat hurts."

"You were injured. Bad," my wife said and, quietly, unemotionally, told me what she knew about my stepping on the IED. She said I kept pointing to my legs (although I don't remember doing so). My pointing caused her to assume I knew I had lost both of them.

Something had happened to me. That was obvious, and I knew I had been badly wounded. I felt as if I had come out of a coma or a deep sleep (which I had), and because of the heavy medication, I felt no pain. Oddly enough, my right toe throbbed—something I would learn to call phantom pain. That may have been why I kept pointing to my legs.

As Rosemarie talked, I became aware that my parents were in the room with her. So were my sisters and my brother—the whole family. Rosemarie says I smiled, closed my eyes, and went back to sleep.

> I became conscious of Rosemarie talking
> to me. Nothing sank in until she said,
> "And you . . . you lost both your legs."

The next time I awakened, or at least the next time I was alert, I stared at my family. The expressions on their faces made me sense something really bad had happened to me.

Slowly I became conscious of Rosemarie talking to me. Nothing sank in until she said, "And you . . . you lost both your legs." Her tear-filled eyes stared at me.

"No! No! I have my legs. I can feel them."

By then my left hand had been amputated, and I didn't know that either.

"Your left hand—it's also gone."

"No, no, look at it!" I said. "It's covered but it's there!"

I'm not sure what anyone said immediately after that. At the time, I was so excited to be alive, I didn't care. Either then or later, I pulled back the sheet and raised the hospital gown. I saw the stitches. Then, like any normal man, I looked down and realized that my penis and testicles were there, so I relaxed.

But as I stared at my stomach, immediately I thought of the last time I had been with my family, before the Marine Corps deployed me to Afghanistan. That Sunday, all of us went to church together, and that meant a lot to me. We were members of Capilla Cristo Redentor, a Hispanic Assembly of God congregation.

Because we were so close to Fort Bragg and many military personnel worshiped at our church, Pastor Francisco Soltren always included prayers for the military. On my last Sunday, a visiting preacher, Leonardo Mateo, was the guest speaker. After his sermon, he called Rosemarie and me to the front. He didn't know us and couldn't have been aware that I was going to be deployed within the week. "I feel God nudging me to pray for both of you."

Rosemarie and I looked at each other as if to ask, "Why us?" Everything in our lives was fine.

"I sense that both of you are going to experience a very, very difficult time. It will impact your relationship and your marriage. But if you remain faithful, God will take you through."

Although I appreciated his praying, I didn't get it. Our family was blessed and happy.

Pastors Soltren and Mateo as well as other leaders in the congregation came up, and as is common in our church, they anointed Rosemarie and me with oil and laid hands on us. When Mateo touched me, he did something odd. He placed his hand on my stomach. "I feel like praying for your stomach. This is where you need it." His words were powerful and loving, and I sensed God was in his prayer.

When I woke up in the hospital and saw my abdomen and

all the stitches, it reminded me of that day. Lord, I thought, maybe that's why he put his hand on my stomach.

"You had exploratory surgery," Rosemarie said. "They opened you up to make sure your organs were all right. And they are all fine."

I smiled, believing not only that God had led Pastor Mateo to pray that way but that his prayer and those of the others had kept that part of me from harm.

Later, doctors took skin from my stomach as grafts for my hand. My body is filled with scars and reminders of the many skin grafts. But I keep reminding myself, I'm alive and healthy.

I was happy to be alive. With my family present, I had a lot of support.

My brother leaned down and said, "Many people are praying for you. Everyone at your church and at my church."

Several friends had traveled from Puerto Rico to visit while I was still in the hospital. My family was like that—no matter where I was, they visited me in New York, Connecticut, Florida, or Colorado. They gave me the support and strength to keep moving forward. Many times I felt as if I failed them, but they never condemned me.

A few friends from my growing-up years in Puerto Rico also visited. Especially I remember Jose Medina Ricky. It was the first time he had traveled out of Puerto Rico, and he brought his guitar with him and played and sang for me. Efrain and Sheila Rivera, Juan Carlos Tolentino, and Luis Carino, all friends from childhood, made the trip to visit and to encourage me.

Yes, yes, God, thank you because you've put so many godly, caring people in my life.

This Is Progress?

Rosemarie

At the Navy Lodge inside Bethesda, the Marine Corps provided a room for me and for Carlos's parents. We were told, "You may stay here as long as your husband remains in this hospital."

That was such a relief to me, knowing we had a place to stay. I slept well that night—better than I would sleep in the nights ahead.

By five o'clock the next morning, I was outside Carlos's room. Orderlies were getting ready to wheel out his gurney to take him back to the operating room because they still had to cleanse his wounds. The reason for my going so early was that they couldn't take him until I signed the consent form. As soon as I signed it, they took him away.

After they finished cleansing Carlos's wounds, they took him to the ICU, where he stayed two weeks. Until the fourth day, he remained connected to a ventilator. Even though I understood and had been around such situations in my hospital experience, I also knew what could go wrong. He looked so helpless (and he was, of course).

When they took out the tube, I felt relieved. Now he would be able to talk. Even though he could speak, his throat was raw, and to say only a few words was a strain. But he could speak—that was the important fact. And in those days, every bit of progress, no matter how minor, lifted my spirits.

"Carlos!" I said. "You are going to get better. You're in bad shape, but you're going to get better. And I'll be here with you every day."

Carlos's eyes fluttered, and he stared at me. "Rosemarie?" The word was spoken softly but loud enough for me to hear.

I squealed in delight. "Carlos!" I said. "You are going to get better. You're in bad shape, but you're going to get better. And I'll be here with you every day."

At Bethesda, the ICU arrangement was different from hospitals where I had worked. They allowed family members to stay in the room with their loved ones. Other hospitals allowed only one or two family members in for brief periods during specified visiting hours.

It was such a relief being able to remain by his bedside. I stayed there around the clock and left only to hurry back to my room, shower and change clothes. Then I was by his side again.

Once Carlos began to talk without effort, one of the first things he said was, "You have to check on the insurance."

I had no idea what he meant, so I said, "You're in the ICU, so why are you thinking about insurance now?"

"I want you to gather all our important papers."

"Why?"

He didn't explain, but to be sure I understood, he said, "I want the power of attorney, my will, statements from our bank accounts, and our insurance papers."

Carlos had always insisted that whenever I traveled back to Puerto Rico, I should carry those papers with me. "I brought them to Washington with me," I said. "They're in my room."

He smiled.

"But why do you need them?" His asking for them made me feel uncomfortable, but he refused to explain.

Even after I assured him I had brought the papers to the hospital with me, he didn't stop asking. "Is everything in place with the insurance? Do you have the latest bank statements?" He confused me by his insistence. If I hadn't been under an emotional strain myself, I probably would have understood.

The next day I asked again. "Why is the insurance so important?"

He stared at me for a few seconds before he said, "Because if I die I want to make sure that I have everything covered."

I brushed away my tears and kissed his cheek. "Baby, you're getting better. You aren't going to die. I wouldn't lie to you about that. Everything will be fine, so why are you so anxious about things like insurance?"

After that, he calmed down and no longer asked about the papers. I was touched that he was more concerned about taking care of our daughters and me than he was himself.

⤳

After two weeks in the ICU, they moved Carlos to a private room on the fifth floor of Bethesda, 5 East Wounded Warrior Unit. Shortly after we arrived, the head nurse came up to us and introduced himself as Manuel Santiago, Lieutenant Commander, Retired.

"I'm also a pastor and I'm from Fajardo—"

"That's where we're from—"

"Yes, I know. And if you need anything—anything—you ask." Manuel told us that he had made sure we had the best room on that floor. "I know you'll have lots of family coming, and I want to make sure there's room for them to visit."

After that, Carlos's room seemed full of people—relatives and friends from many places. Manuel (by then we were calling him Manny) came every day and several times during the day. He became a pastor to us as much as a nurse, always willing to listen to any concerns we had.

"Now, Rosemarie, you need to take care of yourself," Manny said to me many times.

"I know." But I didn't think much about me. My concern was for Carlos, and sometimes I skipped meals and had no appetite. I'm a small woman and weighed 105 pounds; before long I was down to ninety pounds.

One day Manny walked into the room with a paper bag. He took out a bagel and handed it to me. "Enough of this. Eat this bagel! I'm not leaving until you do," he said and watched until I finished. "If you're not in good condition, you can't take care of him."

He was right, and I knew it. After that, I made sure I ate every day and rested at night. My weight slowly crept back up.

At first Carlos did well, but then the nightmares and hallucinations began. For example, he would be talking about our house or his car and then abruptly he would point upward. "Look! Look at the ceiling! There's something there."

"What is it?" I asked the first time.

"Blood! There's a lot of blood. Blood is everywhere." Then he screamed, "They're coming to kill us! Right now!"

His behavior disturbed me, but I didn't worry. I knew a little about post-traumatic experiences. Each time, I touched him gently. "You're safe now. You're going to be all right. And we love you."

And he relaxed.

6

The Way It Used to Be

Carlos stayed in the hospital, and the weeks passed. The flashbacks and hallucinations didn't stop. They became less frequent, but they still disturbed him.

Although Carlos was my first concern, I needed to see my daughters. Almost every day I cried in frustration, trying to figure out how I could be with him and still care for my two children, who were with my parents in Puerto Rico.

After weeks of separation, I called my mother. "I can't live like this. I have to see my daughters." I spoke to Nairoby on the phone that day, and hearing her voice made my emotional ache even worse.

"I'll bring them to you," she said. The Semper Fi Fund bought a ticket for my brother Hector Diaz so he could help my mom travel with the girls. They flew to North Carolina, where we lived. Friends drove them to Washington, DC, to be with Carlos and me.

I had no place for them to stay because I had only one room. My mother took them to our home in Richland, North Carolina. My tears flowed when they left, but I reminded myself that I had seen them.

Not long enough. Any future visit would make me say, "Not long enough."

After the girls left, I couldn't stop thinking about how our
life had once been. I can't explain the emotions, but I knew
I needed to see the house again. Perhaps it was the need to
restore some sense of normalcy in my life. I knew only that if
I went back to familiar surroundings, it would make me feel
the way I did before Carlos was hurt.

**Home. It wouldn't be the same, but
at least I was away from the hospital
and medical care for a few hours.**

To see our house again became an obsession. So one weekend, family members stayed with Carlos, and I made a quick
trip to North Carolina.

Home. It wouldn't be the same, but at least I was away
from the hospital and medical care for a few hours. Not only
did I check up on everything, but I also picked up the large
accumulation of mail. One of the first things I spotted was
the last letter Carlos had written to me in Afghanistan.

I tore it open, saw the date, and began reading. Then I
spotted the picture of his left hand wearing his wedding ring.
I burst into tears, unable to help myself. I wasn't crying over
his injuries—I had already done plenty of that. I kept saying,
"Right up to the end, he was thinking of me and the girls. He
loves us."

I thought of that last phone call on May 15—the same day
he wrote the letter after he called to say he loved me.

As I gazed at the paper in my hands, it was shocking to

stare at a hand Carlos no longer had. I fell to my knees and praised God for answering my prayer, which had been, "Bring Carlos back home to me."

He had come home. He was alive.

7

Finding Comfort

Like many women, I felt it was my responsibility to lift Carlos's spirits and always be calm when he was awake. The wonderful staff took care of his every medical need. I did nothing—or so it seemed—except sit by his bedside.

During my daily vigil, I found relief in remembering our childhoods; it helped me remain calm and at peace. I reminded myself that God had brought us together. Both of us had believed God had a purpose for us and would use our lives.

I couldn't focus on the future because I didn't know what to expect, and when I did, feelings of inadequacy crept over me. So instead I dwelled on the days before the accident. Our childhoods. Our dating. Our wedding. Our family, and certainly our church families in Puerto Rico and in North Carolina. Carlos and I had so much in common. It seemed natural that we'd be together.

When our birthdays rolled around, we used to laugh. "We were born the same day," Carlos loved to tell people.

"Really?" they'd ask.

"Sure, just a year apart," he'd add, and smile. It was true. He was born October 17, 1979, and I was born on the same date in 1980. But that's not all. Carlos has a twin sister, Carla—so all three of us share the same birthday.

Carlos and I have known each other since we were children. I was born and raised in Fajardo, Puerto Rico, a small city on the Atlantic Ocean.

Carlos was also born in Puerto Rico, but his father was a merchant marine and traveled a lot. The family moved to New Jersey, where Carlos stayed until he was four years old. Then the family returned to Puerto Rico. Carlos didn't know Spanish, and since the classes in elementary school start in Spanish, he had to repeat first grade. That put him in the same class I was in.

It seemed like we had been friends from the first day he came into my classroom. That's probably not true, but I couldn't remember a specific introduction. Carlos liked being around my family. Because his father worked long hours and was often away, Carlos didn't get to see his dad much. Seeing my father with his kids was something Carlos missed, and he admired that about our family.

The biggest difference in our childhood was our church experience. From the age of four, my parents took me to a Pentecostal church, Iglesia Cristiana de la A la Z. By the time I was twelve, I could say, "I'm a believer," and was baptized in water.

My family's church was very evangelistic. Every week our members went from house to house to talk to people about Jesus. Some people considered me a fanatic; I thought of myself as committed to God, who wanted me to preach and urge people to turn to him.

In fifth grade, I took a box of New Testaments to school and gave them out to the other students. One day I put the remaining New Testaments in a circle on the ground, and I preached to any kid who would listen.

Carlos told me, "That's when I began to notice you. No

one else stood up for Jesus Christ the way you did." Another time he said, "I especially remember when you preached from Matthew 24 about the end time."

That always made me smile. Our pastor had delivered a powerful sermon, and it was so memorable to me that I used the parts I recalled to preach to my schoolmates.

A few times Carlos imitated me standing in front of the other kids, ignoring their taunts and snickers. He meant it in fun, not out of meanness. "If you accept Christ, he will be with you forever!" He raised his right arm, insisting that's what I did. "If you don't accept him, you're going to hell."

He had been raised in the Reformed church and had never heard anything quite like that. "I don't want to go to hell," he told me.

That part I remember because I prayed for him.

Shortly afterward, his friends Tamara and Sonia invited him to a Baptist church—a charismatic type of congregation. The pastor ended the service with an altar call and Carlos raced to the front. Carlos liked telling me that part. "You got to me first, and I was hooked." He turned serious then and said, "I committed my life to God. And when I did, I felt something I'd never felt before, and I knew it was real."

Despite his experience, Carlos's mother made him continue to attend the Reformed church. And he became actively involved and worked closely with pastor Ruben Santos.

Carlos and I saw each other during those years, but we didn't do any dating. He stayed in the same church until he was nineteen years old, and he became the church's youth pastor.

We even saw each other at a youth organization in our high school. Most of the students, like me, came from Pentecostal churches. His best friends urged him to go to their church, La Confra. That church was different from anything he had experienced. They spoke about being baptized in the Holy Spirit and speaking in unknown tongues.

Carlos's pastor insisted they were wrong, but as Carlos later said to me, "I saw the difference the experience made in the way those friends lived—more committed and more serious about God—and that appealed to me."

His faith made a difference in his life then, and I prayed that his strong relationship with God would help him now.

In one of my low moments, I went back to the time when Carlos and I began to develop a relationship. Peace would come over me, and if I closed my eyes, I could see that face of his, constantly smiling. Even in school, he was the friendliest kid I knew.

We saw each other occasionally, but when I was in the eleventh grade (by then, Carlos was a year behind me because I skipped a grade), one of my close friends, Yaritza Mateo, told him, "Rosemarie really likes you."

Carlos was surprised—but not disappointed. He contacted me and we talked for a long time. We started with our younger school days, which led up to our commitment to Jesus.

Shortly afterward, Carlos's twin sister, Carla, his brother, Raphael, and his older sister, Yessenia, all had conversion experiences and joined the Pentecostal congregation, Iglesia Misionera Emmanuel Defensores de la Fe.

I graduated from high school and entered the University of Puerto Rico in Humacao, and Carlos and I lost track of each other. Upon earning my undergraduate degree in nursing, I went to work in a hospital. From friends I learned that Carlos had gone to a Pentecostal Bible college in Trujillo Alto, called Colegio Biblico Pentecostal—about a forty-minute drive from our hometown.

~

One day, while home in Fajardo visiting family and friends, I decided to do a little shopping and walked into a Kmart.

"Hello, Rosemarie."

I spun around, and a grinning Carlos threw out his arms and hugged me. As he embraced me, I realized how much I had missed him. We hadn't established any kind of love relationship, but I'd always liked him very much.

As I learned, Carlos was zealously involved in youth ministry all over Puerto Rico, and he had helped organize several churches.

I listened to his adventures and smiled. *What am I going to say to him about my own life?* Like many college students away from home, I had slowly drifted from the church. I hadn't intended to push God out of my life, but it happened. A decade earlier, I had been the one serving the Lord, and Carlos had been on the outside.

He mentioned that he had been thinking about going into the military—the Marine Corps. I shrugged. "If that's what you want, go for it."

He stopped talking and gave me a wonderful smile. "And what's happening in your life?"

At first I couldn't look at his face. "Not much . . ." And then the words flowed as I told him the truth. As I continued to make excuses for myself, I could see he was disappointed. "So right now," I said, "I don't have much of a relationship with the Lord."

He didn't condemn or preach to me, as I would have done to the other kids when I was in fifth grade. Instead, we talked about general things for a few minutes, and then I told him I had to move on.

I don't recall our seeing each other again after that. At least not until after he was in the marines.

One afternoon I must have been frowning as I remembered the guilt I felt over moving away from my faith. I was leaning on the side of Carlos's bed, lost in my thoughts, when Carlos awakened.

"What's wrong, baby?" he asked. "Don't worry. We'll be all right."

"No, it's not that," I said. Then I told him I had been thinking about the time we met again in Kmart. "I was so ashamed of myself. I had failed the Lord and myself. And I disappointed you—"

"But you're here now, and we're both serving the Lord, aren't we?"

I smiled and nodded. "I don't know what I'd do now if I didn't have faith in him."

Carlos
I remember that morning well. And I wanted to comfort her. I wasn't physically able to do anything, but with my right hand, I gripped hers. "I love you, and we're together."

I recalled that day in Kmart but didn't want to focus on it. So instead I started talking about my time in the Marine Corps. "When I enlisted, this wasn't the kind of life I expected."

She nodded. "So much has happened since."

"I don't remember the exact day I first considered enlisting, only that it was in April of 2004. I was watching TV and they showed action photos of marines fighting the first battle of Fallujah, Iraq. 'I should be doing that,' I said. That thought wouldn't leave me. 'I should be there.' Then I asked myself, Is God speaking to me? Is this the Holy Spirit leading me?"

I paused to look at Rosemarie, and the pain had disappeared from her face. She smiled and nodded.

"Even now, in this bed and this condition," I said, "I believe I did the right thing."

"I know you did." She kissed my forehead.

"As an American citizen, I felt a strong, patriotic duty to be part of the fighting force in the Middle East. I go could there as a Christian and serve the Lord at the same time."

"And everybody discouraged you," she said.

"Not so much discouraged, but several friends tried to talk me out of it. And the more that people tried to explain why I shouldn't enlist, the more convinced I became that it was what God wanted me to do. Nobody believed I would actually enlist.

"I enlisted in December 2004 and was sent to boot camp on Paris Island, about five miles south of Beaufort, South Carolina."

I stopped and told Rosemarie something I hadn't mentioned before. "Most of the other recruits were eighteen and nineteen years old. At age twenty-four, I felt like an old man among those young guys. No one said anything, but that's the way I felt. And I worked hard to keep up with them."

"The weather was cold then, wasn't it?"

I laughed and nodded. "South Carolina *is* the South, so I thought the weather would be like Puerto Rico. I don't think I ever got warm during my three months of basic training."

Both of us laughed, realizing how much we had both learned about winter in the South. Then I thought of the special letter my brother, Raphael, sent me while I was in boot camp. "Reading that letter was special for me. I was cold, shivering, and wondering why I had enlisted."

I had read one paragraph so many times I could quote it from memory, and I did so as I lay in my hospital bed: "'Wherever you go and whatever you do, remember, you don't need to wear a uniform to feel like you're someone. You *are* someone, and you are the one who is giving value to that uniform.'"

"After that, whenever I went through a hard time—and marine boot camp is tough training—I'd repeat those words. I kept on and made it through basic training. By then, I knew I wanted to be a marine, and I liked being part of them.

"And even now, I still want to be a marine." As I said those words, though, I knew it was no longer possible for me to serve my country.

Rosemarie kissed me lightly on the cheek. She didn't say anything, but then, she didn't need to. She understood.

Rosemarie

"And after that, you came back into my life," I said. "You didn't forget me."

Carlos smiled, and his studious expression told me he was remembering how we reconnected. He took the initiative—I would have been too ashamed.

"Yeah, I never really got you out of my system. You were the only girl I thought about. I met a number of attractive women, but none of them were you."

"Is that right?"

He squeezed my hand, and I smiled because I knew it was

true. For Carlos, there had never been anyone else. In contrast, I thought I was in love once, but it didn't work out.

"The next time I heard from you was during your the third deployment."

"In Iraq," he said. "The longer I was gone, the more I thought of you. And prayed for you. The feeling kept growing.

"I looked you up on Facebook. Because we had the same birthday, I sent you birthday greetings, and you replied. We kept the back-and-forth dialogue going for quite a while."

"Then you stopped."

"A tactical error," he said. "A bad one. But we were so involved in strategic operations that I did little but eat, sleep, and go out against the enemy. I thought of you every day. I prayed for you, but when I returned to the barracks, I was worn out. Sometimes I fell into my bunk and didn't awake until reveille.

"When I got back to Puerto Rico," he continued, "you were the first person I called."

"And I wasn't home."

"And I was really disappointed," he said. "That afternoon I decided to go shopping at Kmart."

I smiled, remembering. "A voice called out, 'Rosemarie.' Even before I turned around, I knew it was you. You hurried over to me, hugged me, and kissed me."

"Can we—can we get together?" he had asked.

"I don't think so," I'd said. "I'm mad at you."

"Why?"

I could tell he didn't know.

"You contacted me while you were in Iraq, and I liked that, and then you called me several times. But without warning, you stopped calling, and I never heard from you again until I see you here today."

"I'm sorry," Carlos had said.

"I believed you," I recalled. "I knew you, and your words softened me."

Carlos was home for two weeks, and we spent as much time together as we could. During the hours I was working as a nurse, he spent time with his family.

We smiled at each other, remembering that carefree time of early dating.

"You told me I was beautiful. That melted my heart."

"Even more. I told you I wanted to marry you."

"Oh, I remember!" I said.

Both of us giggled.

"Your exact words were, 'I *know* you're the woman I want to marry. I've never loved anyone this way.' Then I told you I was back in church, serving the Lord, but I didn't feel I was 100 percent committed."

"I said I'd help you get all the way back," he added.

"And you did."

Minutes passed in silent, warm reminiscence. Then Carlos kissed me, and it felt like we were back in the time before May 15, 2010.

Several minutes passed in silent, warm reminiscence. Then Carlos kissed me, and it felt like we were back in the time before May 15, 2010.

We talked about our marriage and how wonderful everything had been. This time of remembering was something we both needed. It lifted my spirits, and it helped Carlos focus less on his pain and more on our love and the Lord's presence.

I told Carlos, "Right after the wedding, you whispered to me, 'This isn't just a commitment to each other. It's also our commitment to serve the Lord.' And you were right."

Carlos fell asleep, but I continued to reflect on the excitement of the days after our wedding. Three months later, I moved near Camp Lejeune in Jacksonville, North Carolina. Carlos was already in the process of buying a house there for us.

As I pondered that time, I realized that once I fell in love with Carlos, I also fell in love with God again. "I want to serve you," I told the Lord. I confessed all my wrongdoings and weakness. I knew he had forgiven me.

Now, sitting beside my wounded husband, I once again affirmed my commitment. "Thank you, Lord, for bringing us together. And thank you for bringing me back into fellowship with you."

One of the first things we did once we both were in North Carolina was to join a church. It was where we belonged, where we could begin to serve God.

Then came Carlos's assignment to Afghanistan. It surprised me. Three times in battle areas already—surely he had earned the right to be deferred from yet another dangerous deployment.

"I'm a marine," Carlos said. "We don't go to the safe places. We go where we can make others safe."

After Carlos left, I went back to Puerto Rico to be with our two families and to raise our children in that environment. I took a nursing course, prehospital trauma life support, never realizing how helpful it would be. There were even classes about bombs, amputations, and the lasting effects of such trauma. I wasn't conscious of taking the course because Carlos was going to Afghanistan. Yet now, looking back, I smiled. "Yes, God, you were preparing me for the days ahead. Please, please don't let me forget."

Most of the time I was able to remember.

⌒

I still couldn't take care of the girls while Carlos was in the hospital, and my mother couldn't stay indefinitely in the States, so I talked to my close friends, Zoe Cruz and Keira Acevedo in Fayetteville. "I don't know what to do," I said. "Can you take care of them?"

"Yes, we can do that." Both seemed eager to do anything they could to help.

That relieved me, but leaving my daughters was heartbreaking for me. Though I knew it wasn't logical, I felt guilty for my inability to care for my two babies. I could see them only twice a month at most, and even harder, I had to split them up. More than once I said to myself, I'm the worst mother in the world. Because my duty and desire was to be there and care for them, I felt torn and tormented every day, and I kept trying to figure out some way to change things.

Had I done the right thing? Should I have stayed with the children at home and visited Carlos on weekends? I considered it, but staying with Carlos seemed like the right thing. Yet the guilt never left me.

"God, give me peace. I'm doing the best I can."

And the peace came—for a time.

8

How Much Can I Take?

For three months, Carlos remained in the hospital, and for three months our daughters were with someone else. It was a difficult period for me, trying to be both the faithful wife and the loving but absent mother.

I knew I belonged exactly where I was: daily at Carlos's side. Yet even though my in-laws were with me, I felt lonely at times with no close friends around. Regularly I called my friends on my cell phone. That helped—but it also hurt. The worst time each day was when I asked Zoe and Keira in North Carolina about my children. My heart broke every time I heard the reports. "Where is Mommy?" Nairoby never stopped asking.

Every day I spoke to her on the phone, but I'm not sure how much she understood. She wanted me there. "Why can't you come home right now?"

"Mommy's here with Daddy. Mommy loves you," I said. "Daddy is very, very sick and I have to be with him, but I'll come to see you soon."

That was my struggle. I needed to be the wife, but I was missing out on being the mom.

Most days I was an emotional mess. Carlos's hallucinations didn't go away. Despite my prayers and those of our family and friends, nothing really changed. If he was getting better, I didn't see it.

One day I reached the utter breaking point. Carlos's hallucinations and nightmares had gotten to me. The tears began, and I couldn't stop them. I sat beside his bed, desperate, and the sobbing grew worse.

"Oh God, I can't take any more," I cried out. "This is too much. He's still hallucinating, and he doesn't seem to be making any progress. Please, God, how much of this will I have to take?"

Then the tough questions hit me. *Will it always be like this? Will those things torment him the rest of his life? What will it be like with our daughters growing up and hearing him scream like that?*

"God, how much longer is this going to continue? I'm worn out, and he's not improving or getting beyond those horrible nightmares. I love Carlos. You know that I love him. But I'm just not strong enough to handle much more of this. Please, please help me."

Though I couldn't hold back my tears, I didn't want Carlos to see them. I looked around and figured his bathroom would be a safe place to cry. Without thinking, I grabbed my iPod, turned it on, and sat down on the toilet seat.

The tears didn't stop, but then the music from my iPod broke through my pain. It was a beautiful song in Spanish, reminding me that God's grace sustains us and makes us stronger.

I stopped crying and listened to the words. Then I played the song again . . . and a third time . . . and a fourth. God was using the music to speak to my broken heart. The song ended with a prayer asking for God's peace.

By then the tears had stopped. I turned off my iPod and sat

in silence, asking the Lord to forgive me for wanting to give up and for telling him I couldn't take any more.

A thought came to my heart, and I believe it was God: "To quit is not your decision. It is mine."

A thought came to my heart, and I believe it was God: "To quit is not your decision. It is mine." That made the tears flow again, and I asked him to forgive me and strengthen me for whatever Carlos and I had to go through.

Immediately, strong passages from the Bible flooded my mind, some of whose locations I didn't even know, such as, "You [God] will keep in perfect peace those whose minds are steadfast, because they trust you" (Isaiah 26:3). The verse that lifted me most was Psalm 23:4: "Even though I walk through the darkest valley, I will fear no evil, for you are with me; your rod and your staff, they comfort me."

God's peace flowed over me. The tears were gone, and I knew—I truly knew—I could keep going.

A few days later, doctors discovered the medications for pain were causing Carlos's hallucinations. Once they switched to a different kind of med, the hallucinations stopped. God had answered my prayers.

June 13 was our anniversary, and I wanted it to be a big event for Carlos. My sister-in-law Yessenia was visiting. "I want this to be really special for Carlos," I told her.

I decorated the room, brought in balloons, and even put up a banner. Champagne has been an anniversary tradition of ours where we both lived, so I bought champagne flutes. I still have them.

"Will you go to the Cheesecake Factory for me?" I asked Yessenia. It was the nicest restaurant I could think of near the hospital. "Bring us the best dinner they have on the menu."

"Yes," she said. "If you like, you and Carlos can have dinner alone."

I invited a few friends; however, Carlos was in isolation. That meant they had to put on the sterile gowns and gloves. As strange as the party looked—as if all of us were in costumes—we celebrated.

Once again I pushed away all anxieties and worries.

9

Up and Down

Carlos

During those terrible early stages of my recovery and adjustment, the presence of our head nurse, Manny, often felt to me like I was being surrounded by angels. God put that man there to take care of me and of Rosemarie. Manny seemed to grasp our hearts in a special way.

We had many other wonderful support staff as well at the hospital. None of them ever treated what they did as merely a job. Until then, I never knew so many good people were out there. They cared about us, and although they didn't say a lot, their patriotism showed. The therapist, the doctors—everybody—was very, very supportive. In my best moments, I felt good and so grateful.

I had to accept that it wasn't going to be a fast recovery, and I learned to take each day as it came. Some days I felt good; I also had many bad days. One of my worst times was when I ran a fever for two months. The doctors thought it was an infection because my left leg wouldn't heal completely. Rosemarie figured it out and said to the doctors, "Maybe it's not an infection but a reaction to the medication you're giving him. Why don't you change the medication?"

The doctor did exactly that. He ordered a new medication. By the next day, all my fever was gone, and it didn't return.

About a year after my injury, I developed a small open wound in my leg from HO (heterotopic ossification). I had problems with the bone in my right limb. After an amputation, the bone can grow. I thought it was nothing and didn't mention it to the doctors.

After two to three weeks my right leg began to stink, and I started running a fever. The limb turned red. When Rosemarie showed the doctors, they told me I had an infection in the femur, and they might have to amputate more of my right leg. I put further amputation out of my mind, refusing to consider that possibility.

> I had to accept that it wasn't going
> to be a fast recovery, and I learned
> to take each day as it came.

That was one of the worst days of my life in the hospital. They began giving me antibiotics and other medications; treating the infection kept me in the hospital an additional ten days. "You caught an infection from the blood transfusion you received in Afghanistan," the doctor said. "It was probably what we call dirty blood—not 100 percent pure."

I wish he had stopped there, but continued, "From that dirty blood, you might end up with HIV or hepatitis."

The possibility of HIV upset me so much I started yelling. I looked at Rosemarie and I screamed, "God! Where is God? God, where are you? Why me? Why is this happening to me?"

I received no response from the Lord. That truly was the

worst moment of my time in the hospital. But as it turned out, the transfusion hadn't caused any damage. Thank God, the infection didn't get to my bone, and after ten days of treatment, I was free from that threat.

When I talk about that experience, I say, "That was a very, very, very bad, very bad day."

Another time, as I was lying in bed in Bethesda receiving a transfusion, my face became red and my heart rate went up so rapidly I could hardly breathe. Rosemarie was there, recognized what was happening, and called a nurse.

The nurse stopped the infusion and said, "Something is wrong here." She checked the blood type again and it was fine. They didn't know what was causing the problem.

"We need to take you back to ICU," the nurse said, "so we can watch you carefully."

"Oh, no." I groaned. Silently I asked the Lord, "How much of this must I endure? Will I ever get out of here?" For me it was like stepping backward. As they wheeled me back to ICU I kept thinking, I'm not getting better; I'm getting worse.

Oh Lord, help me. You saved my life in Afghanistan, and now I'm going to die here!

I didn't die and was released from ICU. That's how my life went for the first months—up and down.

Up and down.

I want to be clear that not everything was bad during my hospitalization, and the staff did everything they could to make my stay easier. One of the things for which I'll always be grateful was my visit by wounded warriors.

While I was in Bethesda, several marines visited me. I hadn't known any of them, but that didn't matter. These wounded warriors—veterans who were further along in the recovery—spent time with me. Most were equipped with prosthetics. Their purpose was to encourage by example— and it worked.

One who encouraged me the most was Todd Nicely, a quadruple amputee. He had lost everything—both legs and both hands. But when I looked at his face or talked with him, not once did I detect self-pity or anger. His attitude shouted, "I'm alive! I enjoy my life!" He was one special, special inspiration to me.

Another wounded warrior I'll never forget is Brian Kolfage, who was air force. Like me, he had lost both legs and a hand. And like Todd Nicely and all the other wounded warriors, he was excited to be alive. Several times, Brian and his wife came to visit me in in the Marine Wounded Warrior unit, third floor, at Bethesda.

The first time I stared at his prosthetics. Brian smiled and said, "Sergeant Evans, this seems very, very hard, and it is, but you can get over this. And you're going to do it! Don't give up!"

As I looked at him and understood what he had gone through, I silently asked God to give me the courage and faith to hang in there the way Brian and the others did.

Brian's example gave me so much hope. *If Brian can do this, I can too.*

As orderlies were taking me into Ward 57 one day, I saw David Lyon, the explosive ordinance specialist I'd worked with in Afghanistan, lying in a bed in the same room. "What happened to you?" I asked.

That's when I learned about the second blast I had heard while I was being medevacked from Afghanistan. Like me, David had stepped on an IED, and like me, he had lost both legs.

Sad and as shocking as the news was, we didn't talk about IEDs and injuries. Both of us wanted to focus on getting well. From that day on, we trained together to get strong enough for prosthetics. We did it competitively, and our friendly, daily contests enabled me to change my focus to getting better.

There was more than just a growing relationship between David Lyon and me. His family and mine encouraged each other. My mother and David's family bonded and became very good friends. It made me realize that when you're in the hospital, you look for someone you can relate to, a support system.

Few men in Ward 57 were as determined as David to get out of the hospital. His optimism pushed me. He made it out before I did. I was happy for him, but I missed his cheerful challenges. However, I was better and more optimistic about my own recovery.

David was from California, so he eventually transferred to the Naval Medical Center, San Diego, usually referred to as Balboa Hospital because it's located next to Balboa Park.

We stayed in contact. Then in 2015, I received word that David had died of a cardiac arrest. I wept when I heard the news. And though it wasn't reasonable, I felt guilty, as if in some way I had put him in the situation where he stepped on the IED.

The staff at the hospital did all they could to help me get better. I was, am, and always will be grateful. They were ready to attend to whatever wounded warriors needed. But one thing they weren't equipped to do was take care of my family.

10

A Family United

My goal was to walk using prosthetics. That meant that I had to start physical therapy and heal my legs. After three months, they transferred me to a room. The hospital provided a hotel suite for Rosemarie in the Malone House, which was attached to Walter Reed. We also learned that I would need to stay in the physical therapy program for two years.

They weren't set up to accommodate families and we understood. But being separated from our children for two years was more than we could handle emotionally. We prayed often—daily—about how we could have our daughters with us. "Lord, show us what to do," was our constant prayer.

Rosemarie missed the girls more than I did. I was in therapy for hours every day, and Rosemarie was there for me, watching and learning ways to help me. But she thought constantly of Nairoby and baby Genesis. She didn't say much, and I knew it was because she didn't want to upset me. But in my best moments, I could see the sadness in her eyes.

God, please, please help us find a way for all four of us to live together.

Most of my surgeries took place at Bethesda. In July of 2010, within three months of my injuries, I was moved into a private room at Walter Reed for my therapy. That was a big day for me. I was making progress, and that lifted my spirits.

Many celebrities came to my room. They were kind to us wounded warriors and told us how much they appreciated what we had done for our country. One of the first visitors was the first lady, Michelle Obama, who really made me comfortable in her presence. Drew Brees, the quarterback for the New Orleans Saints, visited. Almost every day a celebrity came to see us—baseball players, actors, and also politicians such as Secretary of Defense Robert Gates. They came to encourage us, and I enjoyed meeting them all.

But the people who mattered more to me were my family and my friends. And the best part of my move was yet to come.

⌇

"Are you ready to see your daughters?" Rosemarie asked me. "They'll be here tomorrow."

I should have been overjoyed at the prospect, but I wasn't. I wanted to see them and to be with them. But I didn't want them to see me like this—a man with no legs and missing a hand.

"When I start walking—"

"Nairoby wants to see you," Rosemarie insisted. "Every day she asks when she can see Papi again."

My wife was right, of course. And eventually both children would have to see me as I was. I still didn't like it.

They were still living in North Carolina, and Kheyra

Acevado and her soldier-husband, David Vaillant, brought them to see me one Sunday. Before they got there, they talked to Nairoby and explained what happened to me.

Even so, I was nervous when she came into the room. My heartbeat sped up. I think that I was afraid my daughter would reject me. Rosemarie helped her get into the bed with me and put baby Genesis on my other side. Nairoby sat down, and I hugged her. I was very emotional because I was scared. I really didn't know how she was going to react to me.

She hadn't seen me since I left for Afghanistan. Every day I had thought about her countless times. She had grown so much since then, and I commented. She smiled.

I asked her how she was.

"I'm fine, Papi," she said matter-of-factly. "How are you?"

"I'm fine too." I smiled at her and gave her a big hug.

She started telling me about games on her Nintendo and then about her friends at church.

"Papi's sick right now," I said, "but Papi's going to be all right."

"I know, Papi."

She continued playing and talking and then stopped. "Papi, Papi, you don't have no legs." She said it calmly. She wasn't asking me or showing surprise, simply stating a fact that she had finally grasped.

I started crying, feeling so much self-pity.

"It's all right, Papi," she said calmly. "Don't cry." She went back to playing and talking to me.

Abruptly I stopped crying and feeling sorry for myself. That's how kids see it, I thought. They're so innocent and accepting. I had worried that she might reject me or be upset because I had no legs, but for Nairoby it wasn't a big thing.

Rosemarie
Whenever friends visited from North Carolina, I begged them
to bring the girls. After the visit, I realized they were happy to
do that, delighted they could do something for me. Each time
the girls came, my spirits buoyed, and I tried not to think it
was only temporary. *They are here now. We're a united family again.*

The best part of the girls' coming was that they were able
to see their daddy and spend time with him. With each visit,
they adjusted, probably better than I did. It was as if this
was normal for them. As they played, and Carlos relaxed and
smiled with that wonderful grin so characteristic of him, I
felt better.

> With the Lord's help, I knew Carlos and
> I would stand together no matter what.

Bigger battles were yet ahead for us. But with the Lord's
help, I knew Carlos and I would stand together no matter
what.

⟱

I wanted to move to an apartment so I could bring our daughters to be with us, but I didn't know how to get permission
and find a place. Then I realized that just moving into an
apartment wasn't enough. I'd need childcare for both girls
during the day while I was at the hospital with Carlos.

My heart was heavy, and I couldn't believe God wanted it
that way. I inquired of anyone who I thought might know of

an apartment or who could refer me to someone who did. But nothing seemed to happen. And the longer it took, the more discouraged I became.

I didn't know it, but God was already sending us the answer through a hospital volunteer named Heather Bernard. I'll never forget her.

The details are vague, but Heather came into the hospital room when Carlos was asleep. "How is he doing?" she asked.

"He's coming along," I said. "Slowly." I probably said more, happy to have someone who wanted to talk to *me*.

She smiled as she listened. When I finished, she said, "And you? How are you doing?"

"All right," would have been the normal answer. But that time, I sensed she cared and had asked seriously. I tried to open up to her in language she would understand. "Even after they discharge Carlos from the hospital, I've been told we have to stay near the hospital for two years."

"I think that's normal for people like your husband."

"But that's not the hard part." I told her about our daughters living so far from Washington, DC. "I want to see my girls and have them with us. I need to find a place for us to live until they release Carlos."

She listened and asked sensible questions about what kind of accommodations we needed. "I don't know the answer," Heather said, "but I'll keep asking until I find out who does."

I believed her. Hope filled my heart, and after she left I prayed, "Lord, is Heather the one you're going to use to answer our prayers?"

Heather visited regularly to tell us about the progress she was making. One day she burst into the room. "Are you familiar with a nonprofit organization called Operation Homefront?"

Neither Carlos nor I had heard of it.

Heather explained that Operation Homefront, founded a few months after 9/11, provided assistance to families of wounded warriors. She had been in touch with them and was sure they could provide us with an apartment "large enough for all four of you."

Carlos and I cried, hardly able to believe what she told us.

"Because it's a nonprofit organization, they depend on donations to pay for their services. In other words, if they can help you work this out, it won't cost you anything."

Heather connected us with Operation Homefront. They state that they are a national benevolent organization. On their website are these words:

> *Mission:* Build strong, stable, and secure military families so they can thrive in the communities that they've worked so hard to protect.
>
> Operation Homefront is a national 501(c)(3) non-profit whose mission is to build strong, stable, and secure military families so they can thrive—not simply struggle to get by—in the communities they have worked so hard to protect.*

Their website continues by spelling out the programs they offer:

> *Relief* (through Critical Financial Assistance and transitional housing programs), *resiliency* (through permanent housing and caregiver support services),

---

* "Mission and Impact," Operation Homefront, accessed March 15, 2019, https://www.operationhomefront.org/aboutus

and *recurring family support* programs and services throughout the year that help military families overcome the short-term bumps in the road so they don't become long-term chronic problems.

Heather asked Felucia Suluki from Operation Homefront to contact me. Felucia did more than contact me. She found us an apartment.

I was overjoyed until I saw the place. "But—but it's on the fourteenth floor of an apartment building. How can that work? My husband is in a wheelchair." I wasn't thinking rationally.

"There is an elevator, although I would think only the worst that could happen is that it might not always work," Felucia said. "Other military families are here."

I apologized and admitted that it had been unreasonable of me to object. "I've been living purely on emotions."

Felucia nodded. "It's all right. This is a huge emotional issue for you."

She helped me realize that the apartment would work for us, and they would charge us nothing. She took me inside the building, up the elevator, and to the apartment. I smiled and thanked her again and again. "Yes, yes, it will be large enough for all four of us."

Friends from North Carolina helped us moved in on Friday, August 20, 2010—three months after the accident.

Carlos

Although many wounded veterans lived in the complex, I would become the first triple amputee. Despite all the good news, part of me resisted—and my thinking wasn't clear in those days, which may have resulted from all my medications.

"What's the catch?" I asked. "Who provides anyone with a free apartment for two years?"

Felucia explained that Operation Homefront was a non-profit organization, and their money came from caring people who donated funds for wounded warriors.

"And we have to pay it back later?" I asked. "Is that right?"

"No, no. It's a gift—our gift to warriors like you who gave themselves in service to their country. We feel it's an honor to help you."

"Okay," I said and thanked her. Even though I knew all that, I had to hear her explain everything to break down my resistance. But I also realized something: I still wasn't open to letting people help me. I'd always done everything for myself, or at most, I had gotten help from family members—never from strangers and never from asking for assistance.

But I was learning, and I grew in my appreciation of the many people who did so much to help me lead a normal life.

11

What Kind of Man Am I?

About the time Operation Homefront gave us the apartment, I finally realized I had been focused on myself, and poor Rosemarie had it worse than I did.

I couldn't drive—which was one of the things that troubled me the most. I couldn't do errands. Inside my head, I listed all the things I could no longer do.

Rosemarie had to do everything; I was helpless.

My uselessness lowered my self-esteem. I didn't feel like a real man. *I don't know if I'm going to be able to be the husband that I promised her to be. I don't know if I can be the father that I promised the girls to be because I can't. How am I going to support my family?*

I was still fragile, an emotional wreck.

At the apartment, I wasn't in the controlled environment of Bethesda. Even little things upset me. My neighbors and everyone around me had both legs and hands. I didn't want them to see me and feel sorry for me. Except for going back and forth to the hospital, I never wanted to leave our apartment.

Rosemarie
I'm grateful for the moral support within the apartment complex. A number of families were living there through the

generosity of another wonderful organization, Wounded Warriors. Their area director lived in the apartment next to us, and she always seemed ready to help if we asked. Just having her close, knowing she was ready to help, brought me comfort.

Before long I had established a regular routine of waking up early, getting Carlos cleaned up, making breakfast, and then awaking, dressing, and feeding the girls. Every day, Monday through Friday, I drove Carlos in my Mazda to the hospital for therapy; we had to be there by nine o'clock.

Carlos's father and mother came to live with us for a short time, and that was good for him. They took care of the children while I was at the hospital with Carlos. It felt comforting to have both our children with us. We were a family united again.

Yet despite all that, it wasn't easy. I had a routine, but every morning I felt pushed and stressed getting everything ready. By night I was exhausted. I don't think I ever got enough sleep during those days in the apartment. But I reminded myself that all four of us were together.

It will get better. I can endure this for two years.

We faced several new problems, and again caring people came through. Heather put us in touch with the Semper Fi Fund, Operation Second Chance, and St. Francis International School in Silver Springs, Maryland. Representatives from each of those organizations eagerly reached out to us.

One of our first concerns was a school for Nairoby. New friends at the apartment helped us find one that was only a ten-minute drive from our apartment. That was fine in the beginning, but Nairoby had problems adapting. She spoke Spanish better than English, so the language adjustment was difficult. She also needed my attention so she didn't feel neglected at home. Carlos was still seriously ill and needed constant care, but so did our four-year-old daughter. She was too young to understand everything that was going on, and she had been away from us for so long that she needed our assurances we wouldn't leave her again.

And I failed her. Sometimes I even expected her to help me with simple housework, but I knew that wasn't realistic at her age. "But we're a family again. We're together. Together." I kept saying those words to myself.

Then after less than two weeks in preschool, Nairoby's teacher called. "Your daughter began screaming and wouldn't stop. Then she fell on the floor crying." She told me about several other incidents of bad behavior. They weren't normal for Nairoby. But what *was* normal anymore?

"I'll do my best to help her at home," I said, and I tried to explain to Nairoby how to behave. But Nairoby wasn't old enough to understand or articulate her feelings. Her behavior didn't change, and in less than a week, the teacher called again. "Mrs. Smith, who is on staff here, is going to work with your daughter."

Mrs. Smith was the perfect answer for Nairoby. The first day, she said to me, "I know you're already stressed. I want to help you so you don't have to worry about Nairoby. If I can do that, I know it will make life a little easier for you."

I could have hugged her and kissed her. Finally someone understood.

Mrs. Smith gave our daughter a great deal of attention— exactly what Nairoby needed. For example, she brought a teddy bear to school just for our daughter. Within days, Nairoby's behavior improved. In fact, she soon became one of the best-behaved students in the class.

I thanked Mrs. Smith profusely. And most of all, I gave thanks to the Lord for making everything work out so well.

Carlos
Our apartment had three bedrooms and two bathrooms, which was wonderful, especially during the first month when my parents were with us. I was grateful to Operation Homefront for getting us such a nice place.

But I wasn't all right. *What kind of man am I?*

When I was in our apartment and had the energy to do anything, I dragged myself across the floor, pulling myself only with my right hand and my stub of a left hand. That in itself was exhausting.

> I was helpless, and I couldn't shake off the constant reminders of what I couldn't do.

But worse was seeing Rosemarie forced to do everything, even simple things like taking out the trash. In the past, I'd always done that, but now I was helpless, and I couldn't shake off the constant reminders of what I couldn't do. Many times I wondered why God had spared me. *I'm useless and a terrible burden to everyone. Rosemarie and the girls could have a good life if I wasn't in their lives.*

One day I was sitting in a chair, staring out the window from the fourteenth floor. *I could just fall out the window and make everyone's life easier. Once I'm gone, they could carry on without me. Wouldn't they be better off without a legless father?*

I didn't realize how common depression is among wounded warriors, especially those of us who were deployed more than once. In 2017, when I was able to look back, I read an article in *USA Today* with the headline "Suicide Kills More U.S. Troops Than ISIL in Middle East."

"Suicide—not combat—is the leading killer of U.S. troops deployed to the Middle East to fight Islamic State Militants, according to newly released Pentagon statistics. . . . The reasons suicide ranks as the No. 1 cause of service members' death are complex. . . . They probably include . . . post-traumatic stress, multiple combat deployments . . ."*

Because of my depression, I must have been difficult for my family to handle. I didn't know how to pull myself out of my self-destructive mind-set. At times I doubted God's love for me and couldn't conceive of any divine plan for my life.

As a Christian, I couldn't—and wouldn't—have taken my own life. But more than once—in fact, regularly—the idea crossed my mind that I was a heavy burden my family didn't need.

---

* Tom Vanden Brook, "Suicide Kills More U.S. Troops Than ISIL in Middle East," *USA Today*, December 29, 2016, https://www.usatoday.com/story/news/nation/2016/12/29/suicide-kills-more-us-troops-than-isil-middle-east/95961038/.

12

The Problem Was Carlos

We were together and trying to function as a family, but it wasn't easy, because I was the problem. Genesis wasn't old enough to know what was going on. Nairoby was accepting, and to her I was Papi—with or without legs.

Despite that, I cried a lot and continued to struggle with depression.

I was on heavy doses of narcotics for the pain, but the real issue was that I couldn't accept who I was without legs. When we came home from therapy each day, I wanted to go into our bedroom, slam the door, and stay there. Alone. The children's noises bothered me. If they cried, I was irritated and upset. If they were laughing, it disturbed me just as much. Rosemarie was sharp enough to read my moods.

I knew it wasn't right for me to be that way. I was grouchy and made the rest of the family miserable. But I didn't know how to help myself. And prayer didn't seem to work anymore.

Rosemarie

Carlos became increasingly irritable. Nothing pleased him. He had wanted all of us together, but when the children played or made any noise, he'd yell. "They're making so much noise it hurts my head. Can't you shut them up?"

I felt bad. I had yearned for all four of us to be together—to be a complete family. I tried to reason with Carlos. "They're children. They make noise. I know you're sick, but you need to understand that they are kids. They're going to play, and it's unreasonable to expect them to act like adults."

After each outburst from Carlos I'd get away from him and go into another room and pray. "God, you brought him back like this, and right now our family is finally together in an apartment. But nothing pleases him. He doesn't want to be with us."

Carlos admitted he was pulling away, but he couldn't seem to help himself. No matter how much I prayed, he didn't get better or change his attitude.

At the beginning, I was patient and understanding. I reminded myself that Carlos had gone through a lot and was hurting. As a nurse, I knew that medication also affected people and made them angry and depressed.

But as time went on, Carlos's temperament didn't change— except to get worse. Nothing I said or did made him happy. I began to feel like I was the victim. I thought, "I'm doing all the running around trying to be a full-time mother and your full-time caregiver, and you don't appreciate anything that I'm doing. I never have time for Rosemarie, and I don't know how to relax anymore. I don't get enough sleep, and I don't have anyone to care about me. When does this end for me?"

The problems began each morning shortly after five o'clock. And worsened. Carlos didn't want to get up in the morning and yelled at me for waking him. "I didn't sleep well last night," he said many times and wanted to miss his daily ther-apy. But I yelled and nagged at him until he stirred from the bed.

The worst part for me was the feeling that he didn't want to be with the kids. Having them and me with him seemed to mean nothing to him.

After weeks of his bad temper, I began to get mad. It was strange, because I was so angry, wanting to yell at him as much as he yelled at me, yet at the same time, I loved him deeply. Then I'd remind myself that I needed to be strong for Carlos and for the girls. *This family will totally fall apart unless I take care of them.*

"Lord, you have to help me. I'm getting to that desperate place again."

Then God sent Tamara Lopez to us.

Carlos

In October, Pastor Tamara Lopez, who had become a friend, came to visit. She wasn't in the apartment long that day before she saw how bad things were—without Rosemarie having to say anything.

She came into the bedroom, closed the door, and started talking to me. Others had lectured me and exhorted me, and Rosemarie complained, but I kept thinking, I'm the victim. I'm the one who has no legs. I'm the one missing a hand.

Tamara started talking to me, and I tried to defend myself, but she wasn't going to let me get away with it.

"Yes, yes, I know you're in pain, and you hate it. You don't have legs.

"But you're alive. And you have a wife who's here with you. Not all wives would do what she's done. Long before now, many of them would have walked away.

"Also, your daughters are able to be with you. And people keep trying to help you and care for you. But you don't seem to care about anyone but yourself."

No one had spoken that plainly to me. And I listened, even though I didn't like what she was saying.

"You're thinking about yourself all the time, Carlos, and it's not working. If you don't change, you're going to lose your family."

"You're thinking about yourself all the time, Carlos, and it's not working. If you don't change, you're going to lose your family." She moved close to me. "Do you understand that? *You're going to lose them.*"

That hit home. I already knew a number of soldiers, marines, and airmen whose wives and children had left them.

"You're right," I said. "And I don't know how to change."

"God knows how to change *you.*"

Tamara prayed for me and for the family, and then she left.

Her words got through to me. I was ruining everyone's life, and I felt guilty and selfish.

Tamara didn't say much after that whenever she visited. She had said enough.

I wish I could say I had a complete turnaround. I didn't—not then—but I did start noticing how badly I was behaving.

One day I screamed, "I want to quit. I want to die. It's not worth going through this!" My parents were there too, and they saw how bad off I was.

Another time, I had enough control to realize how badly

I was treating Rosemarie and the children. "Why don't you take the girls, leave me, and keep moving forward?" I asked. "You don't have to be with me. You didn't marry me for this. I was supposed to come home well and be a good husband. Instead I came home a cripple."

Tears rolled down her cheeks. "No, no. I love you for who are. You don't have legs, but you're still Carlos, the man I loved enough to marry." She lost control and sobbed.

Then she brushed away her tears, came over to me, and stared into my eyes. "I love you for who you are," she repeated. "You're here with us. I prayed for God to bring you back to us. And God did."

"But I don't have legs, I don't have my left hand, I'm not the person I used to be."

She grabbed what was left of my left hand and began kissing it. She hugged me and kept saying, "I love you. *You!* I love who you are and not who you're not."

That melted me. She demonstrated her love and helped me think of God's powerful love for me. I hadn't been able to love myself because I didn't like this deformed, partial body and didn't want it.

"I wasn't born this way. If I'm not born this way, I don't want this new body."

"I love you."

No matter what I said, each time she repeated those three words. And in that moment, as terrible as I had been to her and the girls, I knew she hadn't stopped loving me.

"I see your wounds and scars," she whispered. "The scars are evidence that you're being healed. And Jesus is doing the healing."

One day my best friend, Albert Andino, visited me. I had met Albert in October 2004 in Puerto Rico at the Marine Corps recruiting center. That was the day we both joined the Marines Corps. He started boot camp in November and I left home in December.

After boot camp, I went to the infantry at Camp Geiger, North Carolina. A friend named PFC Sanchez has a twin brother, also a marine, who was in a nearby Marine Corps school. Sanchez asked me to go with him to visit his brother's school. When we got there, to my surprise, I realized his twin brother's friend was Albert.

"We have the same friends!" I said, and it was a fun reunion. That was the first time that I had seen Albert in five months. We had different jobs in the Marine Corps, so I hadn't expected to see him again. After he finished his school, he received orders to the First Battalion, Second Marines.

A month later, I finished my school and was sent to the same battalion where he was. We deployed to Iraq together three times. For me, Albert became the closest thing to my family away from home. His family became my family, and my family, his. Even now, my daughters call him uncle and his daughter calls me uncle.

On my last deployment, to Afghanistan, I went into a different unit than Albert—the first time we hadn't served together. Both of us felt sad that we were being split up. Before we parted, at least three times, Albert said, "Take care of yourself."

I promised I would—something I couldn't fulfill.

But that wasn't the end of our friendship. And later, Albert Andino would show why he truly was my best friend in the Marine Corps.

Felucia from Operation Homefront talked to me one day. They had provided the apartment for us, rent free. She said, "We're setting up an event next month with dinner. How about sharing your story?

"Most of the veterans there will have different kinds of wounds, such as traumatic brain injury [TBI] and post-traumatic stress disorder [PTSD]," she explained. "We've had amputees share their stories, but you'll be the first triple amputee."

No matter what she asked, I probably would have said yes out of gratitude for Operation Homefront's kindness to us. "Sure, why not?" I said. I assumed it was a small group, where I'd tell the story of my injuries, and we'd sit and talk with some of the other guys who lived in our apartment complex.

She had been casual about it, and I didn't think of it as a big deal. However, I was a little nervous because I hadn't shared my experience publicly. I was trying to absorb what it meant to be an amputee without thinking about telling any-one. In our environment in Washington, I was surrounded by veterans like me who were legless or armless.

That evening of October 28, 2010, I wore regular clothes even though I didn't have prosthetic legs. Once there I real-ized I had been mistaken: it was a big event—a very, very big event. It was a fundraiser, which she might have mentioned, but I never imagined the size. She had called it a gala, which didn't mean much to me. I didn't count, but there must have been at least two hundred people in the room.

I was shocked to see a room filled with people, including highly successful business people, several generals, and other

VIPs. It was a really fancy gala, and I wasn't just sharing my experience—*I was the speaker of the evening.*

That wasn't something I was prepared for. Then I thought, I know I can preach, so I'll stand up and preach. As nervous as I was when I took the mic—and I was sweating—as soon as I opened my mouth, the words flowed.

Rosemarie told me I spoke for a little more than three minutes. I couldn't say because I was so caught up in opening my heart that I had no awareness of time. To my surprise, I wasn't concerned about how I looked or what people saw as I faced them.

I introduced myself and then I told the audience, "I never thought I was going to have a normal life again. I worried about my wife and my family, about what we were going to do next, where we were going to go to—you know, all those worries. Then my wife found this foundation, Operation Homefront.

"There's now peace in our hearts and in our minds. We think about my rehab and about me being able to walk and use my hand. Thank you so much for what you guys have been doing for the Evans family, and for all the other families who are living there—all my neighbors. We are grateful."

Briefly I told them about my experience in Afghanistan, but I spent the last part of the time emphasizing the impact of Operation Homefront Villages and my gratitude for what they'd done for me. My final words were, "I never thought there were so many good people out there—so many good people who wanted to help. That gives us hope to keep going on. It's given us the chance to help others one day. God bless you, and thank you very much."

When I stopped, people clapped—and it wasn't polite clapping. I knew they had heard me and resonated with my words.

Before I left, several people came to me and opened their hearts, telling me their stories, their pain, and how difficult it was for them to come to grips with their "new bodies."

Apparently, someone taped everything I said because the next morning at the hospital, one of the double amputees, Sergeant Major Mackey, greeted me and said, "We saw you on YouTube. You did a good job."

"What are you talking about?" I hadn't realized that some- one had not only recorded it but put it on social media.*

Others had also seen it, and that evening I watched it myself. Even though they were my own words, they touched me. It was the first time I realized I would be able to talk about my injuries and also tell others about the goodness of God at work in my life.

Even though I wasn't yet walking with prosthetic legs, inside I was soaring. I had spoken easily and freely. It was my first time.

I knew it wouldn't be my last.

But I still had a long way to go.

---

* "Marine Sgt. Evans Talks About the Impact of Operation Homefront Vil- lages," YouTube video, 3:10, October 28, 2010, https://www.youtube.com /watch?v=HMUjdRhmMyM.

13

Deep Healing

Before I stepped on the IED, I used to tell Rosemarie, "We're a circle. We defend our children; we defend each other. This is us—and we're going to keep the circle strong." In those days I would say, "We have faith, we have love, and we're going to move forward."

I believed those words then. Even afterward, in my worst emotional state, I knew I couldn't give up. I'd sometimes hear my own words shouted at me: "This is us—we are a circle!"

Now Rosemarie reminded me of that image. "This is us, this is our circle, and we're going to survive and grow. We have faith, we have love, and we're going to push forward."

And one of first things for us to do to strengthen our circle was go back to church.

Rosemarie

While still living in the apartment, I took Carlos to therapy every morning Monday through Friday. Our weekends were free, but we didn't do much on them. So when it came time, I didn't ask Carlos what he thought; I just said, "This weekend we're driving to North Carolina and going to church there."

That's where we knew people and people knew us. It would be like taking him home. We had started buying a house before his second deployment, and I thought it might make Carlos feel better to be in his old, familiar surroundings, even though the trip was a little more than three hundred miles. I received a weekend pass for Carlos so he could leave the area.

Carlos resisted. Several times he said, "I don't want everyone to see me like this."

"We're going!" I said. "You might as well get used to it. This is who you are now. If they loved Carlos with legs, they'll also love Carlos without legs."

He agreed with my words, but it was easy to see he hadn't accepted that fact. He was still going through a difficult time, fighting depression, but I kept telling him, "Your friends still love you. They care about you, and they want to help."

It took a long time to get everything ready, but I didn't mind—reminding myself that we'd soon be home. After I was sure everything was set to go, all four of us went down on the elevator. I got Carlos and the girls inside my Mazda and packed his wheelchair inside the trunk. And we drove straight down I-95 to Richland, North Carolina.

Along the way, we had to stop several times, and the trip took us between seven and eight hours. By the time we got there, I was worn out from driving, trying to take care of both kids, and being sensitive to Carlos's needs. But it was worth the effort.

That Saturday, I drove directly to a friend's house. In preparation for our coming, they had built a ramp, so I had no trouble wheeling Carlos into their house.

We saw so many wonderful, supportive friends that weekend, and I felt restored.

Carlos

Saturday night we stayed with our good friends Sammy and Zoe Cruz, who had been taking care of Genesis. They went to the same church we did, and they were happy to be able to take us with them to the Sunday church service.

Sunday morning we arrived at the church. Part of me wanted to be there, but I was still facing my poor self-image. While we were still in the parking lot, we heard the music. Familiar praises, and I knew I belonged there.

Rosemarie brought the wheelchair around and while I was still sitting inside the car, I began crying. The praise music stirred me up, because it was the kind neither of us had heard for months.

Both of us were touched by the sounds and were eager to join in the worship.

Sammy and Zoe helped me get out of the car and into my wheelchair. They pushed me from the parking lot up to the church. We hadn't told anyone we were coming, because we wanted it to be a surprise.

I still wasn't comfortable being around crowds of people, but Rosemarie insisted that I had to start someplace. And as she had said more than once, "Where better than in my home church among people who truly love us?"

As they wheeled me inside, I kept saying to myself, They'll think I'm a freak. Everyone will be uncomfortable and not know what to say or do. I don't have legs and that will be awkward for them.

We'd barely gotten inside the door when people spotted us and started rushing toward us. They hugged us and praised God for us. "We've been praying for you," was something I must have heard a dozen times.

No one seemed to notice that I didn't have any legs and

was missing a hand. They were hugging me and saying things like, "You're home and you're safe!" "We love you."

My tears started again and they didn't want to stop. I realized that our brothers and sisters in the faith cared. They truly were our friends and accepted me as I was.

Once inside, the praise music sounded more wonderful than ever. I don't know if they were more energetic or simply that I had missed it so much. Every song the congregation sang that Sunday morning made me feel as if it had been chosen just for me.

In the middle of the worship, I felt strongly that I needed to go to the altar for prayer, which wasn't unusual in our congregation. I didn't say anything to Rosemarie but wheeled myself forward.

As I went toward the altar my heart was filled with joy and the tears were happy ones. I don't know if I prayed aloud (probably not), but I kept thanking God. "I know you're real. If you kept me alive, it's for a reason. God, I don't know how to live this new way. I don't know how to live without a hand, and I definitely don't know how to live without feet. I don't know how I'm going to support my family. I don't know if I could be a good husband. I don't know if I could be a good parent. I don't know how to live my life. I don't visualize myself in ministry. But here I am. Help me. And use me any way you want."

I was focused on my imperfections and limitations. As I moved forward, immediately loving members surrounded me, and something powerful happened. The Word of God filled my heart and the Holy Spirit truly became the Comforter that Jesus promised. It hadn't happened before that moment, but then, I hadn't been ready until then.

In ways I can't explain, God spoke to me. I heard his voice

inside my head say, "You're looking at it all wrong. The way people stare at you has become your focus. That means you're caught up in your limitations. Stop being a victim and feeling sorry for yourself. Instead, you need to look at your life through the mirror of my Word."

Immediately I thought of the words of Philippians 4:13, which Rosemarie and I quoted often: "I can do everything through him who gives me strength." Although I had read that verse many times, now it had gotten into my heart.

Other verses came to me. Years earlier I had claimed Mark 9:23 as my life verse. In context, a father brought his demon-possessed son to Jesus and begged him, "If you can do anything, take pity on us and help us" (verse 22).

"'If you can'?" said Jesus. "Everything is possible for one who believes" (verse 23). That verse kept ringing inside my head. I didn't expect or ask the Lord to give me back my legs or my hand. I did ask him for peace, inner joy, and guidance.

Another verse came to me, and it took on fresh meaning: "We know that in all things God works for the good of those who love him" (Romans 8:28).

As I listened to the Holy Spirit whispering those words, I kept saying, "Yes, Lord. Yes, Lord."

> In that moment, I felt God's love fill my
> heart, and I knew my wounded body
> wasn't God's way of punishing me.

Until that moment, even though I never said so to anyone, I had been convinced I was in a wheelchair as punishment for my failures. I had failed in many, many small things. But in that moment, I felt God's love fill my heart, and I knew my wounded body wasn't God's way of punishing me.

I lifted both my arms in praise to God. It was the first time I had ever done that in church.

The pastor and others laid hands on me and prayed. I knew they genuinely cared, and their expressions of compassion melted me.

After I returned to the row where Rosemarie sat, the joy still flooded over me. In our style of worship, people clap and raise their hands. I wanted to clap but I couldn't with only one hand. Rosemarie must have sensed what was going on, so she gave me her left hand, and we clapped that way.

Everyone was standing, but of course I couldn't. That day it didn't matter. In my heart, I was standing tall; Rosemarie and I were standing together.

Reflecting on that experience, it's difficult to put into words what happened to me. I can only call it a breakthrough. I felt the peace of God and his deep love. I knew I was accepted, not only by God but by the members of the congregation.

I am a conqueror through Jesus Christ! I can be anything God wants me to be. I may not have legs, but I am alive.

Then I thought, "But Lord, I'm in so much pain." Because my pain was still severe, I was on heavy medication.

Please, God, help me because you know how much I hurt.

Then I had what I can only call a vision—a vision of seeing myself staring at Jesus nailed to the cross. His wounds. His pain. He didn't complain.

Oh Lord, forgive me. I'm not the only wounded one. You were wounded and in agony.

Then I heard the words, "I did it for you."

That truly broke me.

Since that day, whenever I started getting down on myself,

I reminded myself that my suffering couldn't begin to compare with his. And I'd think, I'm not the only one. Jesus had wounds too, and he died—willingly—so that I could live.

After that we went back to Washington, and I was more focused. I was excited about walking. "If I walk with prostheses," I told myself, "I'll look like the person I used to be." I still had wounds that hadn't healed enough for me to start. I focused on getting well enough.

A few days after our trip back to North Carolina, my wound-care nurse was cleaning me and examining me. From the beginning, she had emphasized that each wound had to be cleaned every two days to keep me from getting infections.

Some days when she was working on me and everything was red, her touch made me cringe with pain. "Sorry, but it's part of the process," she said. "The more you relax, the less it will hurt."

I had a wonderful wound-care team composed of Kara Couch, Lorraine Williams, and Lloyd Kingsbury. I knew they cared and were doing everything they could for me.

One day, which I will remember forever, Rosemarie brought Nairoby to the hospital while Lorraine Williams worked with me. They weren't in the room, or so I thought—but as the nurse did her work, I looked up and saw Nairoby standing inside the door, watching.

Until that moment she had never seen me when I wasn't covered with blankets. That day it was obvious to her that

I didn't have legs, and I began to cry, thinking, Now she's going to be afraid of me. She'll see me as some terrible, disfigured person.

As soon as Lorraine realized why I was crying, she called Nairoby over, bent down, and said to my daughter, "Let's heal Papi's wounds. Can you help me heal Papi's wounds?"

"Yes," she said and nodded.

The nurse put latex gloves on Nairoby's hands, and Nairoby did everything the nurse did. Lorraine carefully cleaned my legs and then helped Nairoby repeat her action. Each step of the treatment, the nurse would explain that if she didn't do that, I would get sicker.

Nairoby looked at my amputated legs and said, "Papi, your feet are round," because they were round on the bottom. It didn't seem to matter how I looked. Nairoby saw me as her father. Just a comment, and she stayed focused on doing her task.

Several times she said, "I'm helping Papi get well."

That made me cry even more. Nairoby was so focused on what the nurse was showing her that she didn't seem to notice. "Papi, Papi, you see, Papi, I'm going to take care of you. I'm going to take care of you!"

"Yes, you are, sweetheart," the nurse said and they continued to work together. That compassionate nurse did exactly the right thing, and I knew I'd never have to be embarrassed or apologize for my legless body again. The people who love me also accept me. They accept my new body. I had been the one who didn't want this body.

14

Trying to Walk

At last I was ready to receive my prosthetic legs. What an unforgettable occasion! My physical therapists warned me that learning to walk with them was a process, sometimes painful, and I would always have an odd gait. "It doesn't matter," I told myself. "I just want to walk."

The prosthetics didn't fit correctly at first, and they caused excruciating pain. But I had been forewarned. "The shorter your limbs, the harder it is to fit you properly," my doctor told me. And soon, following a few adjustments, my prosthetics fit great and I was ready to learn to walk.

Wearing my new legs proved more difficult than I had expected. But the atmosphere in which I familiarized myself with them helped—for I was only one wounded warrior among others. And none of us laughed, snickered, or judged anyone else among us. The spirit of camaraderie made each of us stronger, energizing us to achieve our goals. Everyone wanted me to succeed—and I wanted the same for them. Just being with other wounded warriors kept me aware that I wasn't the only one going through the at times torturous therapy.

We represented every branch of service, and all of us had physical disabilities—which is why we were there. That meant we understood each other, and we could talk about our injuries without shame or embarrassment. Almost automatically, we had become comrades of the Amputee Clinic at Walter Reed, what they call the Military Advanced Training Center (MATC), where all amputees go through their therapy.

Each of us had to endure the slow, painful ordeal of learning how to find our center of gravity, balance our bodies, walk, and use our prosthetics. We were quite a mixture of double amputees, triple amputees, and quadruple amputees, and all of us had lost at least some of our mobility. It was comforting to see everybody in the same room, going through the same thing. Being in the military, we competed against each other in a positive way. I began to think of us as the class of 2010 to 2012.

Watching others who looked worse off than I did, and seeing them working on their own, spurred me to try harder. As I got further along, I did what other amputees had done for me—I encouraged the newcomers.

"You're going to make it," I'd say. "During those early days, I didn't know if I wanted to make it. But I did. And you will too." Even though I was repeating many of the things once said to me, the words were coming from my heart.

"Who's going to be the first one to walk?"

"How many laps can you do?"

"How long did you wear your prosthetics today?"

"Who's going to be discharged first from physical therapy?"

Those are the kind of questions and positive challenges we called out to each other. That's how we motivated each other—never in a bad way.

One of the first things we had to learn at Walter Reed is that not all injuries are the same. Each of us healed in different ways, and we eagerly did everything we were told.

When someone started walking before I did—and that happened—I didn't feel bad. Each of us was on our own healing path. By being together, we learned to care for and respect each other.

Eagerly, and with all the effort I could put into it, I was there each weekday, determined first to stand on my prosthetics and then to learn to walk.

I had a great team. (I assume we all did, because those therapists treated us with compassion.) My therapists were Etaine Norris, Adele Levine, Laura Friedman, and Kyla Dunlavey. *Angels* is the best word I can think of to describe them for the way they ministered to me.

There were others who also helped. For example, Major Tammy L. Hipps taught me to drive. My occupational therapist (OT), Oren Ganz, and Sergeant First Class Reed worked on my left hand.

〜

"When can I walk?" I asked frequently. Like every other amputee, I asked the same, impatient questions. Like the others, I wanted to do it as quickly as possible.

As I've mentioned, the biggest problem in wearing prosthetics is to locate the center of balance. It's not an easy process, but like the others, I learned. However, at the time, I was also taking heavy doses of medicine, especially morphine pills, Dilaudid, Lyrica, and Nexium to reduce stomach acid.

Taking that much medication every day meant I was drugged most of the time, and I had to force myself to keep going because the medications made it hard for me to stay awake and remain focused.

Even then, I knew I could never have made it without

Rosemarie. She forgot about herself and her own needs. She struggled a lot to push me to go to my MATC therapy. She was the brightest star in my galaxy.

I rushed into wearing long prosthetic devices. That was a mistake. Several times, my legs slipped out of the prosthetics and I fell. I wasn't badly hurt, but after half a dozen spills, I became a little more cautious in learning to walk. At Walter Reed, the staff worked patiently with me and didn't make me feel like a failure. My prosthetics team at Walter Reed were Mike Corcoran, Art Molnar, Roger Hamilton, and Jamie Vandesea. The world may never know or remember their names, but as long as Rosemarie and I are alive, we'll never forget them.

"You need a little more work," one of the team said. "We have to put you back in stubbies."

That felt like a serious step backward because I had learned to use stubbies before I received my prosthetics. But they were right—I needed to go to stubbies, which would give me more balance. They're six inches long, and they're the best prosthetics for amputees to learn how to walk and keep our balance. I did well with them, and because of that I rushed into wearing my big prosthetics with the knees.

I paid the price for pushing too quickly by being forced to go back to the stubbies to start walking again. My therapy took more time than I had expected.

That return to stubbies was difficult for me because I was tired of being a marine, and especially a tired marine. I wanted to be home with my family. I was depressed and ready to give up and live in a wheelchair for the rest of my life.

Finally I had progressed well enough that I could stand wearing my prostheses because I had found my center of balance. But I couldn't yet walk independently. The first time I put on my prostheses, I could take only about eight steps before the right leg fell off. I plunged to the ground.

I smiled. Instead of frustration I said to myself, "I took eight steps! Eight!"

On top of all that, I was losing weight and artificial legs don't allow for much weight change. I had to be careful to keep my weight up.

Back in late September of 2010, we were returning from the hospital. When we got to the apartment building, I waited until Rosemarie brought my wheelchair around and helped me get into it, and then I put sleeping Nairoby on my lap.

Rosemarie held Genesis against her chest with her right hand, and with the left she pushed my wheelchair. Then she hit a bump, probably a crack in the sidewalk, and I fell on to the ground and dropped Nairoby.

She wasn't hurt, but I was. Involuntarily I screamed in pain.

Rosemarie looked around for help but no one was in sight. Handing Genesis to the now awake Nairoby, Rosemarie lifted me and, with a great deal of effort, put me back in the wheelchair. I'll always remember she was wearing high heels, and despite the pain I was in, I kept thinking, She's Wonder Woman. My body weight was probably about one hundred thirty pounds, all dead weight.

Not only was the fall painful, but I hurt my right upper

thigh. That frustrated me because I had only recently started learning to use a prosthesis. Immediately I realized that meant I wasn't able to use them until my leg healed.

I screamed, but the pain didn't seem to quit. Rosemarie pulled out her cell and called Felucia, who was at work in her office in the complex. Felucia hurried out and said, "He needs to go back to the hospital."

My parents and a cousin stayed with our girls.

The day I fell in front of my apartment was a discouraging time for me. I hadn't wanted Rosemarie to take me to the hospital because it would delay my recovery. But I had no choice: the pain was agonizing and constant—almost everywhere, but especially in my back.

Having started to use prosthetics, I didn't want to stop or go backward. I wasn't doing well with them, but I had begun, and each time I walked a little farther, and my self-confidence grew. I was on my way to whatever it was that God had in store for me. How could this be what he intended?

"You need to go to the hospital," Rosemarie insisted.

"I'm trying to be a father, and I'm trying to be a real husband. You want me to walk again, don't you? If I don't keep going forward—"

"You've been injured."

"If I go, I'll get behind—"

"You're in too much pain and I'm taking you to the hospital."

She did, and it was the right thing to do. It was hard for me to accept moving backward, but if I hadn't gone to the hospital, I could have experienced any number of long-term consequences.

15

Swimming with Dolphins

Rosemarie

Carlos was alive and starting to come alive. He had been in the hospital and under doctors' care for almost five months. Our birthdays were coming up, and I wanted to do something special in 2010. Something for both of us—something joyful and fun to mark the day.

From other vets, I heard about a nonprofit group called Veteran Airlift Command (VAC), so I contacted them. Their website states, "The VAC provides free air transportation to post 9/11 combat wounded and their families for medical and other compassionate purposes through a national network of volunteer aircraft owners and pilots."*

They offered us a free trip to Key West, Florida! I wanted it to be a big surprise to Carlos. Of course I had to tell him we were going away, but I decided not to tell him where, although I did tell him it would be by air—and it was a free trip.

Carlos

"You know, this will be the first time you're in an airplane again," Rosemarie said, "but it will be a private jet."

---

* "Home/About VAC," Veterans Airlift Command, accessed March 15, 2019, http://www.veteransairlift.org/.

"But where?"

She smiled, kissed me, and said, "A fun place. You'll see."

Despite feeling some anxiety, I didn't say much. How would people treat me? Being around strangers, especially civilians, still made me want to pull back and not be noticed—but how you not notice a legless man in a wheelchair?

This is the real world. I need to get used to people seeing me. Some of them will probably always turn their heads away or refuse to look below my chest.

Prayer helped me, and by the time we landed, I felt calm. This is just one more challenge, I reminded myself several times.

We flew into West Palm Beach. From West Palm Beach, we rented a car and Rosemarie drove us to Miami, where we visited some family, my uncle Angel Evans. From there we drove to Hawks Cay, which is a small island between Miami and Key West. The staff there were military friendly and did everything they could for us.

While we were still at Hawks Cay, Rosemarie planned another surprise. Before my accident I had been athletic and participated in various sports. She bought tickets for us to watch the Miami Heat play.

Although I was surprised and pleased at her thinking, I was also scared. It was my first time in public among a crowd of people, and though I tried to control my emotions, I wasn't doing very well.

"What's wrong?" Rosemarie asked.

I didn't want to tell her. She had brought me there because she knew what a big sports fan I was. But I was too nervous to focus. The longer we stayed, the worse I felt. Finally I said, "I can't . . . I can't take the crowd and the noise. Take me back to the hotel."

She didn't ask any questions. Instead, she helped me get out of the arena as quickly as possible and drove us back to the hotel.

She understood.

We were booked for a weekend in a first-class hotel in Key West.

I was especially excited because one of the major attractions at that hotel was that residents could swim with the dolphins. Rosemarie was ecstatic and said, "Yes, and it will be something different for you." She didn't know how to swim; I knew and then at Walter Reed I learned how to swim without legs. I wasn't sure I could swim with dolphins, but trying it alongside those friendly creatures would be a new experience.

Rosemarie

I was concerned that Carlos would refuse to try swimming with dolphins, but his response pleased me.

"I'm open to the challenge," he said, and the smile on his face convinced me that he was.

Saturday morning, we went to the place where hotel residents could go into the water. The young woman attendant stared at Carlos and said, "Oh, I'm sorry, sir, but you can't go into the water."

"Why not?" I said. "That's why we came to this hotel."

"It's not accessible for the handicapped."

We had built this up to be such a wonderful outing, and I had anticipated the great adventure of Carlos swimming in the water. When the attendant refused to let us in, I couldn't help it. I started crying.

Carlos, disappointed, took my hand. "It's all right, baby," he said.

"But it's not all right," I said, and more tears flowed.

An attendant who was only a few feet away witnessed the scene and came over to us. "It's true you can't swim here, but I know another place where you can. It's set up for the handicapped."

"But it's closed today," the first attendant said. "I'm sorry."

"Let's try anyway," the second woman said. On her cell, she contacted someone and talked for perhaps a minute, then turned to us with a radiant smile. "They're willing to open it—just for you."

Carlos and I hugged each other. With his right hand, he wiped away my tears.

Because I didn't know how to swim, they provided a life jacket, and someone swam in the water watching us. Once in the water, Carlos learned to grab and hold on to the dolphins and play with them. I loved watching the action. Just to see the joy on Carlos's face made the day special for me.

And that wasn't all. Later that day we went parasailing. Neither of us had done that before, and I was scared. But like Carlos, I accepted the challenge. And it was fun.

Carlos

My two safe places had been the hospital and the apart-ment. Our trip to Florida was my first trip out of my comfort zone—and it taught me a powerful lesson. I realized I had been shy—even fearful—about being around people. Now I was ready to stop thinking that being a triple amputee made me some kind of freak.

> ### Playing with those dolphins, I felt I had no limitations—and that's something I'd never experienced before. I was free.

Being in the water with Rosemarie was a wonderful opportunity for us to be together. And swimming with the dolphins was not only fun, it was also a special experience for me—the first time since my injuries that I felt independent. Playing with those dolphins, I felt I had no limitations—and that's something I'd never experienced before. I was free.

The experience was beautiful for me, just seeing how Rosemarie was going the extra mile to give me this moment of peace and tranquility. She had carefully planned everything.

And she had one more big surprise for me.

When I was blown up in Afghanistan, the blast took my left hand and my wedding ring. I felt bad that I hadn't been able to keep the ring, but I was in no condition to think about it while I was still in the war zone.

On Sunday evening, October 17, Rosemarie made reservations for us at one of the hotel restaurants. The evening was special in every way. We ate filet mignon and sat on the terrace overlooking the cove. There was a fireplace in case the evening felt chilly. I didn't know that Rosemarie had told the chef and the maître d' we were celebrating both our birthdays.

When Rosemarie indicated to the waiter that we were ready for dessert, a group of the staff came to the table and sang happy birthday to both of us.

That was fun to have them sing to us. Other patrons smiled and waved at us.

As soon as they walked away, Rosemarie said, "I bought a gift for you and I want to give it to you."

Before I could say anything, she said, "I want to give you a new wedding ring." She handed me a small box and I was excited.

I opened the box and gasped. It was a ring—but it was made out of plain metal. I must have frowned. "Okay," I said and tried to smile. I didn't say it, but inside I was asking, This is it?

I picked it up and inscribed were these words: "This is not the ring—look to your right."

Confused, I looked at a grinning Rosemarie and then to my right and saw a ring box. I opened it, and grinned. She had bought me a new wedding ring—exactly like the one I had lost.

Tears came to my eyes, and she reached across the table and hugged me.

That night I put the ring on my right hand and kept looking at it. These days, I keep the ring on a chain around my neck.

Newlyweds Carlos and Rosemarie, in Rio Grande, Puerto Rico. June 13, 2009.

US Marine Corps
Sergeant Carlos Evans
in Anbar Province, Iraq.
November 2008.

First Battalion, Second Marines, Family Day at the pistol range for Carlos and
Rosemarie. 2009.

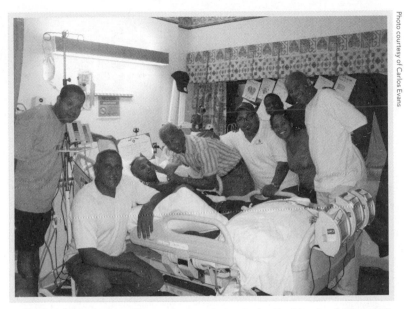

Family members greet Carlos at the hospital in Bethesda, Maryland. May 2010.

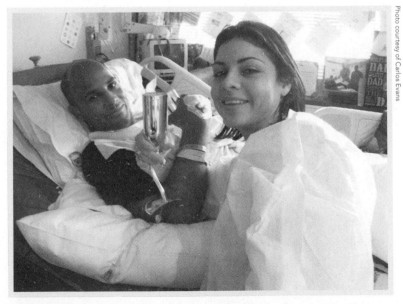

Not even a hospital stay can stop Rosemarie and Carlos from toasting their first anniversary using champagne flutes. Bethesda, Maryland. June 13, 2010.

Carlos and Rosemarie celebrate his first trip out into the sunshine. Bethesda, Maryland. 2010.

Hospital staff and others take Carlos outside for some fresh air. Bethesda, Maryland. 2010.

16

Ski Trip

One of my most frightening challenges took place in early December 2010. I was still involved in the MATC program at Walter Reed. In August my two therapists, Etaine Norris and Harvey Navajo, started talking about going on a ski trip in Colorado sponsored by a charitable organization called Disabled Sports USA.

Before I had a chance to point out that I had no legs, Etaine said, "It's one of our adaptive sports programs. They'll fix you up and you'll be able to ski—"

"Without legs?"

He smiled. "Without legs, and you'll enjoy it so much you'll never miss them."

Rosemarie talked to me about it, and my therapist talked to me about it, but I really didn't want to go because I didn't want to get on a commercial plane. I didn't think I could travel, and I had never skied before in my life. But other wounded warriors who were there talked to me about the trip. And Etaine and Harvey encouraged me to go.

Rosemarie was also invited. Like me, she had never been on a pair of skis, and neither of us wanted to go. "I don't like snow and cold weather," I said. But other soldiers and marines at Walter Reed kept saying, "Do it! You'll love it!"

Then Harvey casually mentioned, "You'll be flying in a private jet and not on a commercial flight."

That piece of information helped me decide. I wouldn't have to be out in public for people to stare at. And even though I probably wouldn't enjoy it, the ski trip would be a learning experience.

"Okay, I'll go," I said.

Disabled Sports USA, a 501(c)(3) nonprofit organization founded in 1967 and based in Rockville, Maryland, serves more than sixty thousand wounded warriors, youth, and adults annually. It is one of the largest national multisport, multidisability organizations in the United States.

On December 4, 2010, about two dozen of us were transported by bus to a private airport outside Washington, DC. We had a therapist with us, and we bonded on the flight.

No one said so, but I think the others without legs were as afraid of skiing as I was. And yet we were excited. The plane landed at Breckenridge, Colorado. For Rosemarie and me, coming from Puerto Rico, Colorado was such a different sight!

Each of us had a private instructor. That first day I met mine—two of them, whom I remember only as David and Michelle. Rosemarie had her own instructor, who was also named Dave.

"Sergeant Evans and Rosemarie, I want to tell you right now," my instructor, David, said with great confidence in his voice, "before the end of this week both of you are going to learn how to ski."

"Sergeant Evans and Rosemarie . . .
before the end of this week both of
you are going to learn how to ski."

I shook my head as if to say, "No, no, no, no I'm not. I don't have legs, I'm missing a hand, I'm not going to be able to do that."

Dave smiled and said, "I'm going to say it again. Sergeant Evans, *in a week* you and your wife are both going to ski."

"Don't get confused because my last name is Evans," I said. "I'm Puerto Rican and there is no snow in Puerto Rico, so this is something new for me."

"You *will* be skiing," he said and ended the discussion. (But he smiled.)

Dave brought skis for Rosemarie, and my David provided a monoski for me—a chair—and it had one blade.

The first thing I had to do was to learn how to use the ski poles to push myself. I was wearing my prosthetic hand so I could hold both poles. Those poles had small blades on them. They were also for me to balance myself while I was skiing.

There were several of us with monoskis. David showed us how to balance ourselves. "It won't come naturally and it won't be easy, but you'll pick it up."

I tried and I fell. I tried again, and I couldn't do it. I have no idea how many times I attempted to balance myself. And it was the same with the other vets. None of us caught on easily.

The next day my back hurt. I woke up, looked at Rosemarie, and said, "I'm not going anywhere."

"Yes, you're going back," Rosemarie said. "You're not a quitter and you can do it."

She reminded me of how wonderful Disabled Sports was to go to the trouble and expense. "And don't forget that David and Michelle promised you that you'd learn to monoski if you kept trying. Don't give up yet."

"Okay, I'll go back," I said reluctantly.

The next day I fell many times again. For the first three days, I was in the snow more than I was in the monoski. But finally I got the hang of it. (All of us legless amputees did.)

By then Rosemarie had gotten so good at the sport that for the last two days she skied by herself. I was doing all right too and skied by myself—although David was by my side to encourage me and to help me if I fell.

On Friday, the morning of our final day, David said, "Sergeant Evans, you are ready for your big solo."

I don't remember if I said anything, but he repeated his words, adding, "I want you to ski down the hill by yourself—the whole way. Alone."

I was nervous about my solo trip but I decided I was going to try it. I had gotten so used to falling, I knew I wouldn't be hurt. I gritted my teeth and nodded.

"You can do it," he said calmly.

I smiled, but it was forced. Not only did I still lack confidence in my ability to solo but I was nervous as I thought about the end of the trip. Yet scared though I was, the challenge excited me. I kept saying to myself, I can do this. I wasn't fully convinced by my own words, but I was willing to try.

David brought all of us amputees to the top of what seemed like a huge mountain. I stared at the view around me; it was beautiful. Pristine snow beneath me, the morning sun shining—I could only smile at the wonderful creation.

Dave helped me get into my monoski. "And now, as you know, this is your last day, and each of you is going to do something on your own." To be sure we knew what he meant, he repeated what he had said earlier. "You're going down the mountain by yourselves. Solo. I'm going down a different way; I'll meet you at the bottom.

"Who's first?"

I was the only triple amputee in the group. It had been a little less than seven months since my injury, which they knew, and I had gotten approval to go. *So why not?*

I raised my hand, thinking I might as well go ahead and get this over.

He smiled and said, "Sergeant Evans, you will not fail."

Every one of us legless vets had to do it, and during the previous days we laughed and kidded each other. I think that was a way of denying how scared we were.

Just before I started, David said, "When you get near the bottom you'll spot several cameras. They'll be recording you." He didn't tell me that one of them would be from Fox News.

Before I started down, I prayed silently, asking God to help me remember everything David had taught me. *I don't want to fall . . . feel confident and yet . . .*

Using my ski poles as David had shown me, I pushed off, and then I was racing downhill. Almost immediately, I understood what athletes mean when they speak of the rush they receive. It happened to me. I did everything as I had been told and had no mishap on the way down.

I felt as if I were flying down the hill. Without help, I finished by myself. I waved and said hello to everyone around me.

A reporter from Fox News interviewed me. It was my first time on camera doing an interview for an international audience. At first I stuttered, not sure what to say, but within a minute I felt comfortable. I knew it was something I could do. Eight months later, that video was posted on YouTube.*

After the interview, David walked over to me. "Evans, look at the mountain."

I did and grinned. "Yeah, yeah, wow, wow! We did it! We did it!"

"Carlos, Carlos, Carlos! *Look at the mountain.*"

"I'm looking."

Now he was shouting. "Carlos, look at the mountain!"

Then it hit me. I started crying. The first day at Breckinridge, David told me I would ski *on my own* by the end of the week. I hadn't believed him. Several times I said, "I can't do that! I'll never do that!"

I stared up at the big, wide grin on his face. "We did it together," I said. "You believed in me and knew I could do it."

Then I said, perhaps only to myself, I'm not sure, "If I can do this—something seemingly impossible and certainly not anything I could have imagined doing—I can do anything." And I thought of Paul's words, "I can do everything through him who gives me strength" (Philippians 4:13).

---

* "Carlos Evans Skiing at The Hartford Ski Spectacular—Disabled Sports USA," YouTube video, 2:32, August 22, 2011, https://www.youtube.com/watch?v=X AXS34kn6bs.

17

Kicking the Addiction

I was taking a lot of medication, especially morphine and Dilaudid.† My pain was so intense they gave me a Fentanyl transdermal patch‡ on my upper chest, which I had to change every three days.

Rosemarie commented once, "I can always tell when you are on your third day."

Surprised by that remark, I asked, "How do you know?"

"You perspire a lot, and you're grouchy." What she didn't say at first was, "And you've become addicted to narcotics."

Although I wasn't ready to admit my addiction, she was right about the moods. The only thing I noticed was having tremors each time before we changed the patch.

Because Rosemarie was a nurse, I used to tell her that she saw the worst side of every pain medication. The medication was working for me, and that's all I cared about.

But not Rosemarie. She worried each time she saw me take anything. Finally—as if holding it back for a long time—she said, "You need to wean yourself away from those meds!"

---

† Dilaudid, a brand name of a semisynthetic morphine drug, is classified as a narcotic. It treats severe pain, and it can be habit forming.

‡ Fentanyl is a strong narcotic used to manage pain that's severe enough to require daily, around-the-clock treatment. It's often used when other pain treatments aren't effective.

"I need them!"

"It's normal that you have so much pain." Her voice softened. "But you have to start working to free yourself from depending on the medication."

"I'm not depending on it. I mean, right now I need them because I hurt so much."

"I see what it's doing to you. You sleep too much. You're angry a lot. Always tired and never want to leave your room—"

"I know, but that's temporary."

She shook her head. "If you want to continue your life, you can't stay here in your room all the time, not doing anything or seeing anyone."

I didn't like hearing what she said; I wasn't ready to admit how bad off I was. Just then, I remembered one time while I was still at Bethesda. Rosemarie and I were talking, and I felt all right. But within minutes, pain shot through my body. "I'm hurting—get me something!"

"Five minutes ago you were all right, and now you're screaming with pain."

"I hurt! A lot! I want something *now*!"

She called a nurse, who gave me an injection, and within a short time the pain was gone, and I felt calm once again. Peaceful. It didn't occur to me that I had learned to like the medication.

"Carlos, I love you. Please—"

"Don't talk to me. I'm fine."

"You're getting high—"

I laughed. "I'm getting calm."

"You've become addicted," she said. "And this is getting out of control."

I didn't want to hear those words. If I had described my

feelings back in the hospital, I would have said the medication was an escape for me. For short periods, it made me feel normal and gave me hope that I could live some kind of ordinary life. In my escape through the medicine, I didn't worry about anything.

But I didn't have much energy, and I kept wanting to sleep.

After a few weeks at home and with Rosemarie's urging, I agreed to go to the pain clinic and see what they could do to help me get over my need for medication. Rosemarie was very direct and told the doctor about the side effects I was suffering, which I would have minimized.

He was wonderful and listened without making me feel I was a baby for taking so much medication. After talking to us, he gave me a few tests and then studied my chart. "Why do you want to change medication?" He listened quietly while Rosemarie again told him about the side effects.

"I'm going prescribe something different, and it usually has fewer side effects. It's called Suboxone."* As he explained, it would help decrease my need for strong painkillers—or at least, that's how I heard it. Rosemarie could hear what he really said—that it would help me overcome my addiction to morphine.

"That's fine with me, sir."

"But I can't start you on Suboxone immediately. First you'll have to stop taking all your current medications for twenty-four hours. That means no narcotics of any kind." He looked at me, wanting to be certain I understood.

---

* Suboxone is for the treatment of opioid dependence.

"Twenty-four hours? Yes, I can do that."

"Remember," the doctor said as we prepared to leave, "you can take absolutely no narcotics for twenty-four hours."

I smiled, thanked him, and assured him I could go that long without medication. I had never used drugs of any kind before my accident, never experienced withdrawal, and had no idea how dependent I had become since I had lost my legs.

"It won't be easy," Rosemarie said to me as we drove back to our apartment.

"I can handle it," I said.

How little I knew about myself.

Rosemarie and I returned to our apartment in Washington, DC, and I was all right. I felt a little pain, but it wasn't bad.

When I went to bed, the pain level had increased slightly, but I was going to sleep. I reminded myself that I had already gone six hours without taking anything.

Rosemarie

Because I was aware that Carlos had become addicted, I knew he would go into withdrawal. I prayed for God to help him, but deep inside, I knew it would be a terrible night for both of us.

About an hour after we went to bed, Carlos was covered with sweat, and he began to thrash about, unable to lie still. He began screaming about the pain. I got up and shut the bedroom door so our girls wouldn't be disturbed. Not only did he scream but he had tremors and diarrhea, and he vomited several times. I refused to give in to my own emotions, determined to keep my voice soft, reminding him that he would get through the night.

"Give me something! *Anything* for the pain!"

"I can't."

"A little. Anything. I need something! This hurts too much!" He yelled at me and screamed again.

He pleaded with me, but I still refused. "You have to go through this," I said several times.

Occasionally I gave him sips of water, but nothing else. "This is a process, Carlos. You must go through this. Just hold on a little longer. You can make it."

"I don't want to make it! I want something so I can stop hurting!"

He kept shaking and couldn't lie still.

Finally I called my friend Tamara Lopez. "Help me! Help me! I can't take any more of this!"

Tamara led us in prayer over the phone. Carlos and I held hands as she prayed. I don't know how long Tamara prayed, but I calmed down and Carlos relaxed. That's the only way I can express it. His pain seemed to ease.

Carlos

After the call, I didn't go to sleep, but I was able to remain calm. It was nearly midnight, and I kept staring at the bedside clock, waiting for six o'clock. By then the sun would be up and Rosemarie could help me get to the pain clinic to start the treatment.

I had no further episodes.

By seven o'clock we reached the pain clinic. And by then I hurt again—a lot. I kept saying to myself, Just a few minutes more. Just a little longer.

Once Rosemarie helped me into my wheelchair, I forgot

about everything except getting relief. I knew I was agitated
and irritable, but during that time, my mind was also clear
and I faced a reality: *I was addicted.*

I turned to my wife. "You were right. I'm addicted to narcotics. I couldn't believe it, but I am."

She squeezed my hand.

The wait at the pain clinic seemed interminable. It was
probably only about ninety minutes, but the pain came back
as bad as any I had felt during the night. I began screaming.
"I need something! I need something for the pain! I need it
now! I can't take any more of this!"

A nurse hurried over to us and asked Rosemarie to wait
while she took me into a treatment room. She gave me sub-
lingual medication—that is, she put a pill under my tongue.
Almost immediately the pain and the withdrawal were gone.
I felt wonderful. And I didn't feel drowsy as I always did with
morphine.

As the doctor explained, it was also a narcotic, but it would
help me. And it did.

For a time.

Like taking the morphine, I became physically dependent on
Suboxone. When we started, I took the Suboxone twice daily
for a time, and finally, once daily. But by now I recognized
my growing addiction. "I need to get off this," I said. "I've
got to beat my dependency."

We both prayed every day for the Lord to deliver me. I cut
the pills in half. I never learned if that would have worked,
because something intervened.

18

Mysterious Bottle

One day I was having a bad time with the pain, and I decided, I'll take an extra one—just one—to get me through.

But I couldn't find my bottle of pills.

"Rosemarie! I need an extra. Just one. That's all I need."

Disappointment showed on her face, but she didn't argue. "I'll get it."

Minutes later she came back into the room. "I can't find the bottle."

"It's a small bottle—"

"I know what it looks like, but I still can't find it."

Together we searched everywhere in the apartment. "They have to be here," both of us said several times.

But we couldn't find that small bottle.

"Oh God, please, God, where is my medication?"

We searched every place two or three times and still didn't find the bottle.

"I need my medication! I need my medication!" By now, the withdrawal pains were creeping through my body. "I need my medication! I have to have it."

By then I was shaking and crying out to God. "What's happening to me now? What are you doing to me?" I cried, and prayed, and even screamed a few times. "Please, Lord, please, help me find the meds! One little pill is all I need."

But we couldn't find the bottle. And the worst of myself came out. I was mad at myself and at Rosemarie. "You lost my Suboxone!"

"You had the bottle in your hand the last time I saw it." She didn't yell, but she wasn't going to let me get away with blaming her.

Then the withdrawal really hit. But to my surprise, the pain wasn't as bad as it had been before. That night I began to shiver and couldn't stop. Rosemarie put hot towels around me. She laid her hand on my forehead several times and prayed for me.

Hours later, I fell asleep.

The next morning, I awakened and looked around the room. *Something isn't right. What is it?*

Then I knew. I felt wonderful. At peace. No pain anywhere.

I remembered something that had happened at church on Tuesday evening, a week earlier. In the middle of Bible study, Pastor Jose Maldonado stopped, looked around, and asked, "Is there someone here who is fighting—trying to quit all medication?"

No one responded.

"I feel that someone needs prayer, and I want to pray with you."

How does he know that I'm going through this? I didn't respond, because I wasn't ready to open myself to everyone. I was too proud to admit that I was addicted and didn't know how to get off the medication.

"There is someone," the pastor said. "I feel this strongly. And I want to pray with that person."

Another minute or two passed before his words finally

touched me. I decided to go forward. Sitting on the aisle in my wheelchair, I pushed myself forward.

He met me, took my right hand, and said, "We're going to pray for Carlos and God *will* set him free."

He prayed, so did I, and probably everyone else in the church was praying as well.

Nothing happened.

No miracle.

I forgot about that prayer. Then that bottle of pills disappeared. And that morning I realized I no longer needed them. "I'm free!" I yelled.

Yes, the prayers of Pastor Maldonado and other Christians had worked. Clearly I was aware that I'd never have to take Suboxone again for my pain. And I never have.

"Thank you, Lord, for making my pills disappear. Now I am healed! I am healed!"

Occasionally I wondered about the Suboxone bottle. What happened to it? It wasn't in the garbage and no one had taken it out of the house. I was free of pain, so it wasn't a big deal. Most likely I wouldn't have thought about it, but it bothered me that Nairoby might find the bottle and take one of them in imitation of what she saw me doing. I told her about the bottle, and she said she knew which one I meant. "If you find it, don't open it, but bring it to me."

"Yes, Papi, I will."

A few days later, Rosemarie was cleaning the house and found the bottle. I had laid it on the windowsill behind the blinds. She didn't tell me, but she took the bottle and hid it from me.

Another week after she found the Suboxone, and feeling convinced I was free from my addiction, she said, "You know what? I found the bottle a few days ago."

"Why didn't you tell me?"

"I'm telling you now because I waited to be sure. You've been without anything for a total of two weeks, so you don't need the painkiller."

"Where is it?" I asked. "Please bring it to me."

She hesitated. "Are you sure?"

"It's all right."

> "I'm free," I said. "The Lord has set me free and now I can serve God totally."

She handed the bottle to me and we went to the bathroom and flushed the remaining pills down the toilet. "I'm free," I said. "The Lord has set me free and now I can serve God totally."

We laugh when we tell that story, because I saw God at work. Even when I wanted to return to my addiction, the Lord loved me so much he wouldn't let me.

Right then I realized that God freed me because he had something for me to do. I wasn't sure what it was, but I knew that I could do it, and I needed to be able to depend only on him.

While on medication, I had wanted to serve the Lord, but I couldn't do anything. I was too tired and often felt like a zombie. The drugs took away pain, but they also took away my joy, peace, and desire to serve.

"You were here with us," Rosemarie said once, "but you

weren't here. Our family was together, and I knew you loved me, but the drugs took away the real Carlos."

"Now I'm back," I said, and kissed her. "For good."

Rosemarie

Witnessing the change in Carlos was amazing. As he became more outgoing, I was able to relax and watch him start being the father and husband he wanted to be. He could do so many things for himself now that he couldn't have done before. He was becoming independent, and that allowed me to devote more attention to the girls.

Carlos

I had learned to ski and walk. But I still struggled with all my limitations—the things I couldn't do.

One day in our apartment in Washington, DC, Nairoby and I were playing. Nairoby was running around, laughing. "Go, run! Run!" I called.

She stopped and said, "No, you run, Papi. You run, Papi."

And right there my spirits sank, and I thought, I can't run. What's she going to think about me? Instead I said, "No, Papi's tired. Papi's not going to run, okay?"

"Okay." Then she ran by herself.

Later, Rosemarie put her in bed. When she came back into the family room, I was crying. "What's wrong?" she asked.

"Nairoby was playing with me, but now she wants me to run, and I can't run. I'll never run."

"I think you're seeing this the wrong way."

"How should I see it?"

"Your daughter is seeing you as Papi. You're the Iron Man. She thinks you can do everything and doesn't see any limitations."

Those words shocked me, but just then I realized Rosemarie was right. Again. To be a good, loving parent, I don't need my legs or my left hand. For Nairoby, it was important for me to be there with her while she grew and learned. So we did things like read a book together. We went through many coloring books.

"She forgets you don't have legs," Rosemarie said.

I grinned and marveled at my wife's wisdom. My daughter was so accepting that, as Rosemarie said, she didn't see my limitations.

19

Others' Marriages

Rosemarie

During the first weeks after Carlos's accident, our concern was his survival and his getting better. In those days, I didn't think much about our marriage. Besides taking care of Carlos I felt overwhelmed trying to be a mother, separated from my two daughters, and my needing to be at Walter Reed with Carlos.

But once our family was reunited and we lived in an apartment, our lives began to take shape, and I thought about our marriage. Part of the reason was that I observed the way other couples related (or didn't relate) to each other.

The hospital set up several occasions for interacting with others. Going there five days a week with Carlos, which included a lot of waiting, I met wives of other amputees. We got to know each other, and in many ways, we formed an informal support group.

"Does your husband . . . ?" was a common topic as we related the way our spouses reacted to amputation, the PTSD, and the medication. Once we got to know each other, some of the women began to talk about their marriage.

I've lost track of the many, many complaints from other wives—and they were legitimate. All of us were under stress, and some more than others. And the stress didn't always depend on whether the soldier lost one leg or was a quadri-plegic. Some people simply aren't built to handle stress. And I want to make it clear right here that I would have been one of them if it hadn't been for Jesus Christ in my life.

No matter how bad things got—and sometimes they were enough that I asked myself if it was worth staying married—I had Christian friends. Members of our home church, my family, and Carlos's family. Not that we told them everything (which we didn't), but I could count on them. I've already mentioned several people God used to minister to us when we didn't know where to turn, such as Tamara.

Carlos and I had a strong, spiritual foundation. Not every couple had that, and stress brought their lack of it to the fore. Sometimes—all too often—those relationships ended in divorce.

"My husband has become a stranger,"
more than one wife said to me. "I used
to know him, but he's changed."

A complaint I heard often was about the lack of intimacy—not just sexual intimacy but the sharing of hearts with each other. "My husband has become a stranger," more than one wife said to me. "I used to know him, but he's changed, and I can't figure him out."

I tried to listen and offer suggestions when I could, but I had my own struggles with marriage. Those two years in Washington, DC, tested our relationship more than any other time.

We interacted with a few stable couples, but only a few.

Most of them were already in fragmented relationships. "We're married, but it's like we're living separate lives," one woman said. "I don't know how he feels about anything." (See the appendix, "A Few Facts About Marriages of Wounded Warriors.")

Some of the wives turned to medication. "I'm deeply depressed," was a common complaint. In time, some of those women became dependent on narcotics.

Other couples stayed together because of the money. The husband would be discharged with full medical benefits, a good pension, and the assistance of wonderful, compassionate organizations that provided a van and often a house. Too often the wives stayed for the security and the benefits. Or sometimes they said, "I'd leave him right now except for the children."

On the few occasions when I mentioned my stress, a common response was, "You should get something to calm you down." They meant prescription drugs—which were available for us.

"No, no," I said each time. "If I start on those narcotics, how am I going to help Carlos get through this? He needs me fully alert." Or sometimes I would say, "I have two very young children. Who's going to take care of them?"

They had answers, but none of them seemed right to me. I would say to myself, God is with us, and he has promised never to leave or forsake us.

My emotions were up and down, and I was aware of it. I once told Carlos, "If I had followed only my emotions, I would have left you. Several times I got to the place where I

told God, 'I can't take any more.' But the Lord always comforted me and kept me going forward."

I heard of one wife who left a note on the bed for her husband
when he woke up. "I can't do this any longer, so I'm leaving."

Another wife left a note that said, "I didn't sign up for this
kind of life, and I can't take it." She left while her husband
was undergoing physical therapy.

I'd hear it as gossip among other wives, as if they were
saying, "She's a bad woman leaving him like that." And yet,
I knew some of them really didn't think the woman was bad,
and they themselves probably would have left if they could.

I don't want to judge them. It wasn't easy for our wounded
spouses, and it wasn't easy for us wives. Only those who go
through such circumstances can truly understand the decisions some of the women made.

But I was determined not to be someone who walked away
from my husband and my promises. When he snipped at me,
when I was exhausted, trying to figure out how to pay the
bills, always I went back to the foundation of our relationship. Perhaps I sound like I'm preaching, but I learned that
we can endure what seems impossible to go through if the
Lord is with us.

God is love, which we all acknowledge, and if our relationship is founded on love for him and for each other, we *can*
make it. No matter what happens, God is still with us. Carlos
and I had each other, our supportive families, and our church
family. That has been the foundation of our life together, and
it has helped us stay together.

Carlos likes to quote Song of Songs 8:7: "Many waters
cannot quench love; rivers cannot sweep it away. If one were
to give all the wealth of one's house for love, it would be
utterly scorned."

20

Return to Our House

Carlos

The first time Rosemarie and I returned to visit our house in Richland, North Carolina, in mid-December of 2010, was seven months after my injury. We were both excited. I'm not sure where my thinking was, but the obstacles I'd have to face didn't occur to me.

Home. Home. That word kept racing through my head.

Rosemarie pulled up to our house, and while she was getting my wheelchair out of the back seat, a shock wave hit me.

I can't get inside my house. In front of me were steps—large steps—and impossible for me to navigate.

Depression hit. I felt like an idiot not to have remembered the steps. I didn't know what to do.

Then I saw my Mustang parked inside the garage. It was a manual four-speed. I stared at it, realizing that I had become a man with no legs and only one hand. "I can never drive my own car again," I said to myself. At MATC I was learning to drive—but I would never drive with a stick shift again.

We had been so excited to see the house again. I had stared day after day at photographs, but they didn't help me face the reality of seeing my Mustang. To some, that may seem like a small thing, and it probably was. But that Mustang had been special to me, a car I loved to drive.

Rosemarie saw me staring into the garage, but she didn't say anything. Instead, she grabbed me, and, as difficult as it must been for her to lift someone twenty-five or thirty pounds heavier than her body weight, she slowly and laboriously carried me up the steps and inside the house. She was perspiring, but she grinned when she put me down. She kissed me on the forehead.

I wonder if anyone can imagine what it was like for me, a normal, healthy marine, to have to be carried by his 105-pound wife into his own house. Humiliating. Depressing.

At the front door, I waited until Rosemarie brought the wheelchair. She didn't try to put me in the wheelchair right there, because it wouldn't have worked. Our door was too narrow. Unable to say anything, I dragged myself into the house.

Once inside, I studied framed pictures on the walls and saw what I used to look like. In the photographs I stood tall; now I couldn't even reach the frame. After my injuries, I had refused to allow people to take photographs of me when they asked permission. If they took them without asking, I always said, "No, I don't want to see them."

In the hospital when other marines came to visit, that had been hard. They were whole and able to walk into and out of the building. They were men who had been with me in combat, and we had been close. But I had shut them out; I could hardly stand to see them in front of me in their uniforms.

While Rosemarie was taking care of our daughters, I began to cry, filling my soul with self-pity. "This is who I've become."

I had seen my house and my car—all the things that used to say who I was—who I had been.

I whispered to myself, "Half the man I used to be." The

experience was so overwhelming, I forgot about God speaking to me in church a few weeks earlier.

A few minutes later, I needed to go to the toilet, and I realized I couldn't even use the bathroom on my own. I called Rosemarie, and as soon as she was able, she lifted me up.

I crawled into our bedroom. From there
I could see our wedding pictures. That's
when I lost all emotional control.

Afterward, I crawled into our bedroom. From there I could see our wedding pictures. That's when I lost all emotional control. The tears flowed, and I couldn't stop them.

I finally calmed down and crawled over to my closet. From the floor, I could barely reach the door handle to open it. Once I swung the door open, I stared at my uniforms. My shoes. My jeans. I'd liked clothes and owned at least a dozen pair of shoes.

Then I stared at an expensive watch I had left when I was deployed the last time. With no left hand, I couldn't wear my watch. It didn't occur to me to think of wearing a watch on my right hand; all I could think about was what I couldn't do. Everything seemed taken from me. It was almost as if the old Carlos no longer existed.

"I can't use any of these things. And this uniform says who I am. These jeans, when I wear them, say who I am. These shoes, when I put them on, point out who I am. Most of all, when I drove my stick-shift Mustang, it declared to the world who I was. This house says who I am now. I can't enjoy any of this."

Right then, God whispered to my heart, "This is not who you think you are. You are who I say who you are. You are my son. You are a conqueror. You are not a victim. Never think that's who you are."

I stopped crying. I didn't have any great experience, but a wave of inner peace came over me. "Yes," I said to God, "I'm still the same Carlos on the inside, and God loves that Carlos."

After that experience, I began to accept that external things didn't make me who I had been or who I thought I was. God made me, he was still with me, and he was reshaping my life. My Maker was now making me exactly the way he wants me to be.

I was determined to learn to look at myself the way he sees me, reminding myself that I can't let any of my possessions blind me to who I am today.

"They don't make me who I am! You, Lord, you make me who I am!"

21

Our Marriage Almost Failed

Rosemarie and I truly love each other and function well together. But there was a point—back before I had admitted my addiction to the pain meds and was still using them regularly—when I thought our marriage might fall apart.

In 2010, I was doing everything possible to get discharged from the marines. I felt overwhelmed, and so did Rosemarie. Despite the good times I had experienced at Key West and in Colorado, in my heart, I still struggled to feel like a complete person, and I felt defeated.

Before I went to Afghanistan, I had promised Rosemarie I would come back, marching on the parade deck. Instead, I returned without legs and missing my left hand. And I was suffering from PTSD.

Even though I could give myself logical reasons, I felt I had let down Rosemarie, my family, and myself. Perhaps worse, I didn't like my new body—and still couldn't fully accept who I had become.

People tried to encourage me, and I received constant support from my family and friends and from my fellow marines, especially those who, like me, had lost limbs. But that didn't help much.

I hate my new body. I'm no longer a complete person.

And yet there were bright times. Whenever Rosemarie drove us back to North Carolina, I was out of the hospital and among people who knew and loved me. I relaxed, and sometimes felt that I was starting to become a normal man again by being with our church friends who prayed for me and loved me. And the presence of family always inspired me, no matter how low I felt.

After the first trip back to North Carolina, I felt much better, and Rosemarie commented on it. After that, we decided that every weekend, Rosemarie would drive us home to North Carolina. (I didn't have therapy on weekends.) Each Friday afternoon, she packed our 2006 Mazda Tribute and drove us to our home outside Fort Bragg. As important as it was to go to our house, perhaps even more significant was that we were able to visit Capilla Cristo Redentor Assembly of God.

Our friends and our family members were close together, and they encouraged us and enabled us to keep going.

Rosemarie liked to drive, and I wasn't yet able to do so. The trip was a little more than three hundred miles and took nearly eight hours, but we did it every weekend. It was good for me and for Rosemarie. In some ways, it helped my wife feel we were easing back into a normal way of life.

We loved being home, but Sunday afternoon was the hard part for us—we had to return to Washington. Each time, it became more difficult to drive the three hundred miles back. We wanted to stay at our home in North Carolina.

Despite the relief and relaxation at home, our marriage wasn't wearing well—for either of us. We weren't getting along as we had before. From my perspective, Rosemarie seemed mad at me all the time, but when I brought it up, she said, "You're the one who's always angry."

She was right, but I couldn't admit it. I couldn't accept

myself. Whenever I stared at my old pictures, I wanted to scream. Many times friends would come around, and I heard them say to Rosemarie, "You're so brave."

In my twisted emotions, I believed she stayed with me only because she felt sorry for me.

"You loved me for who I was, and I'm not that person anymore!" No matter how many times I screamed those words—and I knew they hurt her—she denied she stayed out of pity. I was being terrible to her, but I couldn't seem to change. My actions and terrible attitude pushed her away. I was angry, and in retrospect, I realize I wanted her to be angry too.

Nothing pleased me, and I complained about everything I could. I didn't want her to do anything for me or help me, but she didn't stop. "You're doing everything wrong!" I said that several times. I acted like a victim because I felt like one. And because I could think only of myself, I didn't realize how difficult I was making it for her. Later I realized that, but not then.

Everything I had worked for, especially my career and my family, was lost. I was trying to be normal—but it wasn't working.

The daily stress of being in the hospital and my slow rehabilitation made life worse. Several times I thought I was nearly finished with rehab, and then I'd have a physical setback. I was deeply depressed and wasn't able to admit my despair, and my moodiness upset Rosemarie. Most of all, I didn't like my life, and almost every day I wondered why I was still alive.

Maybe it would have been better if I had died that day. Look at me now—only part of a man. I can't be the father or husband I promised to be. I'm worthless.

The more I thought along those lines, the more I retreated into myself. I didn't want to talk to or see anyone.

Yet every Monday morning, Rosemarie awakened me to get me to Walter Reed Hospital. I didn't want to get up. "I'm tired," I'd say. "I'm still sleepy. The trip tired me."

Like a military sergeant, she said, "Carlos! You have to get up. Now! I need to take you to the hospital. And you are going!"

I was short tempered and very grouchy about her forcing me to get up. My wife didn't deserve to be treated that way, but I couldn't seem to help it. Not only was I upset at Rosemarie, but I wasn't the father I should have been during that period, and I sulked when Genesis wouldn't stop crying.

Despite my struggle with depression, the one bright moment in my day was helping Nairoby with her homework. She was in preschool, and she usually asked me questions. For a short time each afternoon, helping her made me feel closer to her. I think the reason was that it didn't require me to move around and let her see me legless.

The truth is that both Rosemarie and I were exhausted. She was giving so much of herself to me, and I was too depressed to appreciate it.

"The medication is doing that to you," Rosemarie said.

"You think you know everything—"

"I know what Dilaudid does to people. You don't feel pain with it, but it also makes you want to sleep all the time—"

"That's the only time I'm at peace—when my medication kicks in."

Dilaudid is stronger than morphine, and by then I had a pain patch on my chest. When the new patch first kicked in, it was really effective. In fact, I was taking so much of it, Rosemarie told me that sometimes I was out of my head. Yet despite everything my wife said, I remained in denial.

One morning I woke up extremely sick. What remained of

my right leg had turned red, and I was running a fever. It felt like a bone was growing out of my leg.

Rosemarie rushed me to the ER at Walter Reed. The duty doctor said, "It's possible you may have an infection inside the bone."

"Can you give me something for it?"

"Yes, I can give you antibiotics—and I will but . . ."

"But what?"

"We may have to amputate more of your leg."

I didn't cry, but I wanted to. My right leg is only about six inches long, and the shorter the limb, the more difficult it is to wear prosthetics. I knew that if they amputated any more, I would never walk.

They gave me Vancomycin, a very strong antibiotic. I felt worse. Apparently I suffered from some kind of reaction. My whole body started swelling, and my skin turned red. When I stared at my face in the mirror, I looked like a monster.

"Vancomycin can cause the red-man syndrome," Rosemarie said.

I lost all control and all faith. "Where is God! Where is God now? How much more do I have to take? Why me? What did I do wrong? This can't be happening to me!"

Rosemarie started to cry, and the more she cried the worse I felt. Finally I calmed down. "Baby, I'm sorry—"

"I know," she said and let me hug her.

To my relief, the infection cleared up, my condition improved, and they didn't have to amputate any more of my leg.

Rosemarie

In the beginning, I thought I could handle everything. While Carlos was still hospitalized at Bethesda, family members were with us for the first few weeks, and my mom was taking care of the girls in Puerto Rico and later in North Carolina, so I could spend most of my time with Carlos. That allowed me to focus most of my attention on him. By the time they released him, we had our own apartment in Washington, DC.

When Carlos and I moved into the apartment provided by Operation Homefront, both of us were overjoyed. Jordan Hall, the recovery-care coordinator; Felucia Suluki from Operation Homefront; and Semper Fi Fund's Janine Canty arranged everything we needed for the girls. They provided a crib, mattress set, pillows, clothes, and even school supplies for Nairoby.

Heather Bernard, a volunteer from Walter Reed, helped us get Nairoby enrolled in Saint Francis's preschool program.

Our family members stayed awhile and then left after I assured them we could cope. I wouldn't have to tear myself between being at the hospital and trying to care for two young children. I realized that I was suddenly doing the same job a dozen medical people had done at Bethesda.

I thought our lives together would improve; instead they grew worse. Besides being a wife and a mother, I had become a full-time caregiver. Who was caring for me? No one. I didn't ask for help, so I'm not blaming anyone, but my old life had vanished. For the first few months, it felt more like I had a third child than a partner.

Although I understood that Carlos's physical recovery would take a long time, I assumed that by being home with me and knowing how much the girls and I loved him, he would adjust. Of course I knew about post-traumatic stress, but when Carlos's nightmares didn't stop, I didn't know how to cope.

Our life was one hassle after another. I felt worthless because I couldn't do everything. As much as I hated to admit it, several times I asked God, "Is this as good as life will get? Can we never be happy together?"

Although thoughts went through my head at times about leaving Carlos, I couldn't do that. Other couples we knew had divorced, but that would not be our path. God brought us together for life. I thought of the verse in Genesis where it says a man is to leave his parents and join with his wife and they were to be one flesh (2:24).

Life was difficult, but three things kept us together: faith, hope, and love.

Life was difficult, but three things kept us together: faith, hope, and love.

No matter how bad things became between us, I believed God could heal our problems. I also hoped for new medical advances, and prayed that Carlos would get better. I loved my husband and knew that would never stop.

But I also missed the old Carlos, and one day I thought, I'm sure he also misses the old Carlos. He can never be who he was before.

Once Carlos's leg became infected, the doctors told me he would have to stay in the hospital. That's when I fell apart.

I can't take any more! I have to figure out how to divide myself again! I can't be a good mom because I have to be with Carlos. How can I be there for Carlos when I need to be with my kids?

No matter how I thought about it, I couldn't figure out how I could do both jobs adequately. I didn't even think about taking care of myself.

Nairoby was at school in the mornings and Genesis was in daycare, and after I picked up both of them, I returned to the hospital, and all three of us stayed in Carlos's room. Then at night the kids and I went back to the apartment.

The breaking point came.

I can't take any more. I'm worn out.

From the emergency room, I called my mother in Puerto Rico. "I need you here." I told her about the infection and how sick Carlos was. "They may have to amputate more of his right leg. Please, you have to fly here because I need somebody to take care of the girls so I can stay in the hospital with Carlos." I told her I didn't know how long he would have to be there. Because of the tears, I couldn't say anything more.

"I'll get there as soon as I can."

But even that became complicated and added to my stress. Mom missed her flight from Puerto Rico to DC because of a problem between the travel agency and the airline. They straightened things out, but she couldn't get there until the next day. I didn't know what to do. Our church family was three hundred miles away, and it would be a hardship for any of them to travel that far.

"God, I don't know what to do. Help me, help me."

In desperation I called Albert, Carlos's best friend, and explained what happened with my mother. Immediately he left North Carolina and drove to Washington, DC, to stay with Carlos.

I left Carlos alone in the hospital that day until Albert arrived—something I hadn't done before. Unable to take another minute with my depressed and angry husband, I had to get out of there.

Walking and crying as I exited the building, I was absolutely at my lowest point. "I can't handle this. Help me, help," I kept saying to the Lord.

Then Crystal Nicely, the wife of another wounded warrior, Todd Nicely, who was a quadruple amputee, approached me. "You look like you're freaked out," she said.

"I don't know what to do." The tears wouldn't stop. She grabbed me, embraced me, and let me cry until I could talk. "My daughters are here with me, my husband has a bad infection, and they're going to keep him in the hospital. They may have to amputate more of his leg."

"I'm sorry—"

"I need to be there with him, but I don't know what to do with my girls. My mother was supposed to arrive today, but she missed her flight from Puerto Rico, and won't be here until tomorrow. With all I have to do, I don't know how to divide myself."

"Go back inside the hospital and stay with Carlos," she said. "Leave your daughters with me. You can do it. Relax. They will be all right with me."

I stared at Crystal, hardly able to believe what she said.

"It will be all right," she said. "You belong with him. That's first."

I thanked her because she was so supportive. She said, "Carlos's best friend will be with him now."

Her sympathy and encouragement lifted my spirits. Who would understand better than another wife of a wounded warrior?

I passed through that crisis. Carlos and I still had problems, but they were never again as bad as that period. And no matter how terrible I felt or what Carlos went through, we would always be together. God had joined us, and while sometimes it seemed we'd both reached the breaking point, that bond would never break.

Even in those desperate moments, God took care of us.

22

Beyond the Wheelchair

Carlos

When I pause to look back, never could I have imagined what God would do with our lives. I remember lying in the hospital bed, not sure if I would live, depressed when I found I had no legs, and wondering if my life would ever have meaning. I felt God had let me down.

Now I realize God had a plan for me. And this has become a true motto for me: *Now I have one hand, and I'm touching more people than when I had two. I don't have feet, but I'm leaving more footprints than when I had two.*

The Lord has opened doors for me to go all over Latin and South America, Germany, and South Korea. I've traveled from Key West to Alaska. And we haven't stopped.

I'd like to tell you how these travels came about. Although I had volunteered only in my home area and preached in my own church in Fayetteville, North Carolina, I received an invitation to go to Danbury, Connecticut, January 29, 2011, to participate in a fundraiser they called Spin-a-Thon. And the city of Danbury dedicated one day to honor me.

The contact person, and the one who arranged my meeting with Helping Our Military Heroes, was Major Tammy Lynn Phipps. She was on staff at Walter Reed and taught me how to drive as part of their rehabilitation program.

More than a month before we went to Connecticut, on December 18, 2010, I received a wonderful gift—a handicap-accessible van. It was especially adapted for double and triple amputees. Once Major Phipps helped me get used to the controls, driving the van became natural. Having the vehicle and being able to drive again certainly changed my life. That did as much as anything to restore my confidence. I was able to drive and no longer had to depend on Rosemarie or friends to take me places.

"I hope you'll say yes to this invitation," Major Phipps said. "It will do you a world of good to be out there among people—people who care about wounded warriors."

I excitedly agreed for two reasons. First, behind the Spin-a-Thon was a nonprofit organization, Helping Our Military Heroes. They had already raised a lot of money through their Spin-a-Thon. By having me there as a living example, they felt the publicity would raise awareness of the needs of wounded vets.

Three people—Laurie Hollander, president of Help Our Military Heroes, along with her husband, Ted Hollander, and Marybeth Vandergrift—had organized a charity and wanted me to show them the van they had given me. Rosemarie and I drove there. Here's an excerpt from a Danbury newspaper article.

When [Evans] learned that Laurie and Ted Hollander and Marybeth Vandergrift had a charity in Danbury that would give him a van adapted to his needs, he said he knew things would change for the better.

Evans and his wife will drive from the medical center to attend the annual spinathon in Danbury that raises money for the charity Help our Military Heroes.*

The reporter quoted me as saying, "Getting to know Laurie and the others amazes me because I didn't know people cared." And that was true. That event raised my spirits and helped me to look at my life more positively. The article continued:

> "They wanted to help me. It inspires me to do something like that one day. Their giving me the van (will change) my life . . . for the better. Before this, I didn't think I would be able to live a normal life. The van gives me . . . hope."

The writer also quoted Ted Hollander, who said they worked with the Walter Reed Society because "they are able to determine who is ready to receive a vehicle." That meant even more to me—someone at Walter Reed had remembered me and recommended me.

My second reason to go to Danbury was to connect with my grandfather, Carlos Evans Toro, a World War II veteran, who had served in the Pacific. He visited me in the hospital in the summer of 2010. At the time, he was nearly ninety years old and in a wheelchair. I knew it wasn't easy for him to travel at that age, but he didn't complain.

---

* All newspaper quotes in this account are from Eileen FitzGerald, "Danbury Spinathon Helps People Wounded in the Military," *NewsTimes*, January 24, 2011, http://www.newstimes.com/news/article/Danbury-Spinathon-helps-people-wounded-in-the-971075.php.

After his return to Connecticut, he told people about me and my situation. That's when things began to happen. The Disabled Veterans Post 7 in Middletown contributed funds for bringing me there.

*

In Danbury, when my grandfather saw me, he reached toward me and we hugged each other. Our greeting must have been a strange-looking moment to others. We put our wheelchairs side by side, and we leaned toward one another and embraced.

And cried. Both of us. It felt so special for me for us to be honored by Help Our Military Heroes. Chapter 7 of the Disabled American Veterans of Connecticut made arrangements for my grandfather and me to meet publicly. Mike Rogalsky, an army and Vietnam veteran, arranged all the details. As a result, Mike and I developed a warm friendship—and still stay in touch.

My grandfather, who has damaged ear drums and still suffers from post-traumatic stress disorder, announced, "I hope to see my grandson again." (Since then, however, my grandfather suffered from a stroke and has been confined to a wheelchair.)

*

A special event took place that evening with a dinner in my honor and the white table ceremony. Until then I hadn't known about such a ceremony, and now it carries special meaning for me.

No one seems to know the history of the white table. Many believe it began during the Vietnam War. It continued after to honor those who died in the service of their country. Although originally meant for POWs or MIAs, in many places it is now used to commemorate the service of wounded veterans.

Here are the major factors.

1. The tablecloth is always white, symbolizing the pure intentions of those who served.
2. Participants select a small table with a place setting for just one, reflecting the vulnerability of one prisoner of war before the enemy.
3. A single rose in a vase sits on the table, symbolizing the POW's shed blood. The rose also represents the families and loved ones that have been left behind and the faith they uphold that their loved one will one day return.
4. On the bread plate is a slice of lemon as a reminder of their bitter fate. The salt on this plate symbolizes the tears that have been shed by their families as they quietly wait.
5. An inverted glass on the table denotes their inability to be with us.
6. A candle represents the light in our hearts that accompanies the hope that the POW will one day find his way home.
7. An empty chair refers to the reality that he is not here with us.*

---

* See Frederick Brace III, "America's White Table," Veterans Caucus, January 31, 2012, https://www.veteranscaucus.org/america-s-white-table/.

The entire trip was highly emotional for me, seeing a community work together to make me feel like I was at home and that they appreciated my service for my country.

Two days later, on January 31, 2011, the mayor and city council of Middletown invited me to speak at a dinner. My purpose was to thank the people of the city who helped support my grandfather so he could visit me in the hospital.

At a gathering of the Middletown Council on Veterans, Mayor Sebastian presented me with a proclamation "to recognize his service and sacrifice."

Speechless is the best word I can use to express how I felt. No matter how many proclamations, plaques, and awards I receive, it is still nothing I ever want to take for granted or feel it's owed to me. During all those days since my injury, I'm amazed at the kindness of people who honor me. And not just me; I know they're supportive of all us wounded warriors.

> I'm only one of many thousands
> who have given themselves in
> the service of our country.

Many times, even now, I'll be sitting in a restaurant, and someone will come behind me, tap my shoulder, and say, "Thank you for your service" or something similar.

I smile and acknowledge them, and in my heart, I thank God that I'm able to be there to hear those words.

When I speak publicly, I remind myself and my audience that I'm only one of many thousands who have given themselves in the service of our country. And I truly mean those words.

In preparation for the Spin-a-Thon, students at Vinal Technical High School, Middletown, Connecticut, held a fundraising event and collected more than five hundred dollars. Another opportunity for me to thank people and to give thanks to God.

Middletown is grandfather's hometown, and today in the cafeteria where he ate for years, there hangs a photograph of him that expresses gratitude for our veterans' service and sacrifices.

Rosemarie and I spent a special day in Connecticut. Beyond being honored for my military service, that day also helped me feel more comfortable being around people. I no longer felt like a freak.

I didn't do any preaching in Connecticut, but I told them my story and emphasized the presence of God at work in my life even when I doubted him the most. It wasn't a religious meeting, but I wanted them to see my heart and have some idea of my deep gratitude to a loving Savior. The people seemed genuinely touched, and it was a powerful experience for me to see the effect of my words on others.

That day I felt free, the words flowed, and I could tell from the expressions on their faces that they were with me.

Each time I appeared in public, I was becoming more and more appreciative of the sacrifices and gifts of others. Having a van and being able to drive myself did a great deal to help me, but the frequent encouragement of patriotic Americans reminded me that I was serving God by speaking in public. I wasn't sure where it would lead me, but I knew I was doing the right thing with my life in pouring it out for others.

Once I had the van, I drove and preached whenever I was asked. At first I spoke only in our local area, where people knew me. But word of mouth spread, and pastors invited me to preach. By then Rosemarie and I had a Facebook page, and that became the most effective way for people to get in touch with me.

I didn't meet Pastor Raul Feliciano on that trip, even though I knew about him and his ministry. Once I made that connection, it would change the direction of my life.

23

Marathon Man

"You want to run in the Disney Half Marathon?" one of my wounded-warrior friends asked. Before I could answer, he told me it was sponsored by Achilles International.

"It's a worldwide organization where amputees like us can run with the public. Several of us have signed up."

I would be able to use my hand cycle, of course. But a half marathon? That's 13.1 miles. At first, I wasn't too excited about a race that long, and I didn't feel I was that good with the hand cycle to "run" that many miles.

Etaine encouraged me to sign up. "And," he said, "it's an opportunity for you to go to Disney World too."

Janet Patton, a representative from Achilles, called to talk to me, and that motivated me. When I mentioned I was a triple amputee, that didn't seem to bother her, although she said, "We've never had a triple amputee do the Marine Corps half marathon before."

Her statement made me know I had to enter the race. "Then I'll be the first, won't I?"

I reminded myself that the Lord was teaching me I could do "all things." I said yes and signed up for the Disney Half Marathon.

At the hospital, we had bikes, training equipment, hand

cycles and excellent instructors. They wanted us to get a sense of mobility and feel independent. Part of their therapy for wounded warriors was to get us involved in sporting events.

I felt good being a part of a big race in Orlando.

I had to start training, and it was a lot more work than I had expected. I confess that I didn't train as much as I should have.

The purpose of Achilles International is to enable wounded warriors like me, and anyone with a disability, to participate in running events to promote personal achievement.

In partnership with the hospital program at Walter Reed, Achilles International flew us from Walter Reed to Orlando. From the airport, they transported us to Disney World. Some of our family members and friends lived in the area, and they came to the race to support and encourage me. And for me, it was a significant event. Among the spectators were my uncle Carlos, several cousins, and my marine buddy Albert Andino.

We arrived on January 8, and at the hotel I met other wounded vets. I can't begin to explain the peace and camaraderie in being with other amputees.

That evening, we were welcomed by Dr. Dick Traum, the founder of Achilles. In 1976, he ran the New York City Marathon, becoming the first runner to complete such an event with a prosthetic leg. He was a single amputee, having lost his leg above the knee. He also used a hand cycle and promised to stay near me all the way.

The next morning, I was eager to go. I got onto the bike, and I was excited to begin. This was my first race with people other than patients at Walter Reed. Although there were hundreds of regular runners, a minority of us were in wheel-chairs or hand cycles. All of us committed ourselves to run on what the Disney people called "a magical course for the happiest race on earth."

Then we took off. The race was hard—much harder than I had expected. And I paid for not having trained better. Despite that, it was exhilarating to race through Disney World. People lined up on both sides, yelling and cheering us on.

"Go! Go! Go!" I heard that more than anything else, but everyone was yelling words of encouragement.

After about four miles, fatigue set in, and I started saying to myself, "I don't know if you can make it. It's just too tough." I wanted to give up because my body screamed in pain. And that pain never went away during the entire run.

Occasionally, Dick yelled to me, "You're doing great! Keep it up!"

I smiled at him, but it was a forced smile—more like gritting my teeth to keep going.

"I'm here too, and I'm going to keep you going. Don't give up! Keep telling yourself that you can make it to the finish line."

Just then, a runner pulled up beside me and said, "You can do it! You can do it!" He ran beside me and we talked. He was a police officer from Boston, and he must have run beside me at least two of the toughest miles.

"How you doing now?" he asked.

Through sharp, lung-burning breaths, I said, "My first race . . . don't know . . . if I can make it."

"Sure, you can. You can do it!"

"I can! I can!" I yelled back. The truth is that I wanted to quit. But I didn't.

Between his enthusiasm, the cheering crowd, and the presence of Dick Traum, I got past the worst of the half marathon. I probably reached the phase that some runners refer to as getting a second wind.

But my body didn't want to keep it up. Then, just before I felt I couldn't go another mile, I thought of my family. Rosemarie, who was always proud of my achievements, was waiting for me. So were my two daughters. And Uncle Carlos had organized a large family group to watch me.

If I quit, I'll let them down. I have to do this. I must do this.

If I quit, I'll let them down. I have to do this. I must do this.

For the rest of the 13.1 miles, thinking of my family supporting me kept me going.

I finished the race.

I was the last person to cross the finish line, but I didn't care. *I had made it.* Everyone cheered me as loudly and joyfully as if I had been the first.

I did it. I finished the half marathon. Tears filled my eyes, and I reminded myself of the times in the past when I had been certain I'd never do anything like this. The Disney Half Marathon was a powerful stepping stone for me.

Rosemarie and Nairoby kept hugging me, and so did other family members and friends. The Disney people gave me a medal for racing in a hand cycle. Although I appreciated it, for me, it was about finishing the race. I might have been last, but that still means I completed that arduous task.

I did it, Lord. With your help, I did it. Immediately I thought of the words of Philippians 4:13. Yes, Lord, I *can* do anything with your help. I had been persistent, and with the help of those two runners I kept moving forward. Even though I wasn't able to believe in myself, they wouldn't let me give up. I had committed myself to finishing the race, and they helped me do exactly that.

I realized I could do anything I wanted, *but I would have to do it differently.*

At the end of that day, I said to Rosemarie, "I'll never be able to drive again with my feet, but I can drive with my hand." I held up my right hand. "I can do it."

On November 12, 2011, I entered the second annual SWEAT for a VET event, which is held on Veterans Day weekend. It's sponsored by Project VisAbility along with Sport & Health Clubs and other SWEAT-a-thon locations linked through live video streaming across the nation and around the world.

SWEAT for a VET refers to itself as an all-cardio event such as cycling or rowing, an inclusive fitness fundraising event benefiting wounded warriors within the United States and individuals with physical challenges. Here's a reference to me on their website (they showed a photograph of me as well).

"Receiving this hand cycle through the donations from SWEAT for a VET is making a huge difference in my ability to train," said Carlos Evans. . . . Evans is part of the Wounded Warrior Battalion East in Walter Reed Medical Center. "When I was first injured, I thought that I would never be independent or able to enjoy any sports. Now all that has changed. . . . I don't feel my injuries and I don't see that I am missing one hand and two legs. What I feel is freedom. And that is priceless."*

That was the beginning, and almost a year later, several of us hit the Army Ten-Miler with hand cycles. That half marathon at Disney World prepared me—I thought—to enter the Marine Corps Marathon. Had I known how difficult it would be, I wouldn't have signed up. And yet, I'll say that as hard and painful as it was, I felt it was rewarding. It was just one more way for the Lord to show me that nothing is impossible with his help.

* Ali Cierchi and Rachel Zabonick, "SWEAT for a VET Raises Over $120,000," *Club Solutions*, November 22, 2011, http://clubsolutionsmagazine.com/2011/11 /sweat-for-a-vet-raises-over-120000.

Marine Marathon

I completed my half marathon at Disney, followed by SWEAT for a VET. My next challenge was the annual Marine Corps Marathon, held in Washington, DC.

Ever since my first days in the Corps, I had wanted to run in that race, but each time I had been deployed. Now I had my chance, although I'd have to "run" a full marathon with my hand cycle—double the distance of what I had done at Disney World—26.2 miles.

Once again I trained, but afterward I had to admit to myself that I hadn't trained nearly enough. That run was the most challenging thing I had faced since my injury. I was among dozens of wounded warriors competing, and I was with those supported by the Achilles Freedom Team of Wounded Veterans. Altogether, 130 of us competed. Many runners with prosthetic legs passed me within the first mile.

The first negative I faced was the weather. It was snowing—hard. Despite having lived in North Carolina and Washington, DC, I never got used to the frigid temperatures. The cold made my shoulders ache, and my muscles started cramping. I spent so much energy trying to get over the first hills, I wore myself out. My prosthetic hand kept slipping.

The first positive element in the race came from the

volunteers and the crowd of people at every mile of the way. They yelled and cheered us on.

⌁

There are things I would like to share about that experience.

First was the appearance of my best friend, Albert Andino, who is still in the marines. He had visited me many times in the hospital. "Hey, I want to sign up and run with you," he said when he learned I planned to run.

"Too late. It's closed."

"That's okay, Carlos," he said after a brief reflection. "I'll run beside you anyway."

I laughed, not realizing how serious Albert was. He meant those words. He ran up to me just before the race started. "I'm going to run with you."

"You can't do that," I said. "You aren't registered."

"Yeah, I know I'm not, but I want to run this with you anyway. No one is going to pull me out."

"You're crazy! Besides not being registered, you haven't trained for it."

"Doesn't matter. I want to be a part of it, because you're part of it."

He jumped onto the street and began to run right beside my hand cycle. Things went well the first few minutes, and I didn't doubt I could make it. But the longer the distance, the more my self-confidence flagged. So did my physical stamina.

Although I never said a word, Albert called out encouragement from time to time. On two hills, he pushed me so I could make it. After that, he saw I was doing all right, so he slowed down his running, and for a time, he lagged behind.

The snow didn't let up, and the temperatures continued to drop. The harsh wind sucked away my breath. *If I stop, no one will blame me.*

But I couldn't give in. I prayed for strength, I tried to think of God's promises, but I was so miserable and exhausted it was all I could do to keep moving forward.

Remembering the cop from Boston and how helpful he had been, I felt encouraged. And to have my best friend in the race made everything even better.

The 26.2-mile route on the streets of Washington ran past the National Airport, doubling back past the Pentagon and Arlington National Cemetery, and the finish line was at the Iwo Jima Memorial.

Albert ran the entire 26.2 miles, and he did well. I didn't. That's not quite true. I was strong, excited, and made good time—until mile eight. Then I felt as if all my strength evaporated. I wasn't even one-third of the way through and I was already worn out.

My right hand was cramping so badly it felt as if all normal feeling was gone. I wanted to let go of the control and give up. *What did I get myself into? I don't want to do this. I want to quit. It's not worth it.*

"You're not giving up, Evans." Albert caught up with me and yelled as if he were talking to a recruit or had read my mind. "I'm here to see that you make it!"

Less than fifty yards ahead was a steep hill, and I thought, I can't do that one. I can't do it. I'm finished.

Albert reached over and gave me a big push—which others are allowed to do for those of us using hand cycles. With his help, I made it to the top of that hill. That kept me going for a couple of miles.

Another time he said, "I'll push you enough to get you up the hill ahead and then you go downhill on your own."

The cramping didn't lessen and the pain continued to worsen. My breathing became shallower. As I looked at the sidelines, people continued to cheer me on. I gritted my teeth, held on, and kept going.

For another mile.

I'm finished. I can't make it. I'm going to have to quit.

Just then, another marine, a single amputee in a hand cycle, Jimmy King, pulled up beside me. We hadn't known each other—and only after the race did we get acquainted. But it didn't matter whether we knew each other—he was a fellow marine, and he understood my exhaustion. "You can make it!"

Jimmy wasn't the only support—many others yelled greetings and encouragement—but he was the one focused on getting me to the finish line. Instead of "Why don't you drop out?" every voice I heard cheered me on. No competition—just that sense of camaraderie that I'd found in Iraq and Afghanistan.

"I won't let you give up!" Jimmy called out.

I tried to smile, but I was too exhausted to make any kind of gesture. Jimmy must have sensed that. He raced beside me. "I'll help you make it!" He kept yelling encouraging words like that.

To my surprise, Jimmy stayed right alongside me for the rest of the race. A few times I noticed he was perspiring, but it was as if he still had nearly a full tank of energy.

"Relax, buddy," he cried out a few times. "You're trying too hard. Save your energy!"

As I would learn later, Jimmy, also a thirty-two-year-old, was a marine veteran of twelve marathons; this was the seventh time he had raced in the Marine Corps Marathon.

I can't explain it, but I kept going. I don't know how, because every few seconds I would think, I'm ready to give up. I can't keep going.

Somewhere around mile twenty-two, I experienced what many runners refer to as hitting the wall. I was wiped out. Totally. My shoulders felt like lead and my abs ached.

"You can do it, buddy!" King yelled as if he had read my mind. "Hang in there!"

I'll always remember how he cried out, almost like a military command, "You are not giving up! I won't let you quit!"

And I didn't stop, although I still don't know how I revived myself.

At least twice after that, he yelled. "Keep going because I'm staying with you!"

Jimmy pushed me up the hill—again—and he kept right with me, and true to his promise, he pushed me every time I couldn't make an incline.

My spirits buoyed when he yelled, "Hey, Marine, this is the last hill!"

I turned my head around and it was Jimmy King again, pushing me with his hand cycle. "I said you're going to make it!"

That time I nodded.

Still keeping pace with me, he cried out, "Just one more big push and you can make it."

But I couldn't. I gave it everything I had—which wasn't much. I tried going up and slid back down. I tried a second time, still unable to get up the hill. I was frustrated, weak, and kept thinking, This is the end. I've failed.

Something hit my bike. I turned my head around and it was Jimmy King again, pushing me with his hand cycle. "I said you're going to make it!"

I made it to the top, and after that we raced side by side. Together we raced across the finish line. It took Jimmy and me three hours and forty-one minutes to complete the race. People applauded and cheered us for completing. I turned to Jimmy and smiled. We bumped fists.

As soon as we finished the race and I could once again breathe normally, I thanked him for helping me. He and I started talking and we seemed to bond in those few moments.

Jimmy had medically retired in 2006. He had been wounded on patrol while in Ramadi, Iraq, and, for three and a half weeks, had been in a coma. As he told me about his recovery, it sounded like mine. "In the early months, I didn't think it was possible—let alone being able to run a marathon."

I couldn't get over it. Jimmy had slowed down just for me when he could have finished much earlier. But he was a patriot and a true marine.

Christian Davenport, a reporter from the *Washington Post* interviewed us. In his article he stated, "They had started off as strangers, but were now buddies joined in a long hard slog." The article was titled, "Two Wounded Warriors Practice the True 'Semper Fi' in Marine Corps Marathon."*

---

* Christian Davenport, "Two Wounded Warriors Practice the True 'Semper Fi' in Marine Corps Marathon," *Washington Post*, October 30, 2011, https:// www.washingtonpost.com/local/two-wounded-warriors-practice-true-semper -fi-in-marine-corps-marathon/2011/10/30/gIQA6tUTXM_story.html?utm _term=.8e70aa6a781a.

He said it better in those words than I could ever have put it.

Immediately below the article's title was a picture of me and a number of other marines ready for the race. I smiled when I read the photograph's attribution: "Courtesy of Alberto Andino."

—

That race turned out to be a powerful learning experience for me. I thought of the times I hadn't wanted anyone around me, or any help from people outside the hospital.

Each time, God sent someone to push me along. And I realize that's how the Christian life is supposed to work. We do what we can and rely on God using others to push us. "God, forgive me. I do need others."

Through that experience, I was learning not to be afraid of allowing people to help me. Their kind and considerate acts did me a lot of good, and I realized they themselves felt good by assisting me.

Looking back, I realize why the staff at the hospital pushed us to get into those races. The events were part of my therapy. I was getting out in the world again and learning to know people, hear their stories, and it helped me to speak up and tell others about wounded warriors and our needs.

Within a year after my injury, I had not only learned to race with a hand cycle but I learned to swim at the hospital. I had a new body, and I was going to use it.

I got good at using my prostheses. But it wasn't all success. The day came when the prosthetics no longer fit because of my weight change after so much physical training—which, I learned, wasn't unusual.

I focused on trying to look like who I had been. I wanted

to wear my prosthetics all the time so I could wear jeans and look like everyone else. I suppose I was still embarrassed and perhaps ashamed of not being like "normal people." (As I learned in speaking with other vets, that's a common reaction.)

25

Operation Coming Home

While we were visiting our families in Puerto Rico in 2011, a man called me from Operation Coming Home. "My name is David Gaines, and we build homes in North Carolina for wounded vets. Men like you."

As I learned later, someone from the Military Order of the Purple Heart (MOPH), Chapter 2226 of Fort Bragg, contacted Operation Coming Home and told them my story. An impressed David Gaines then called me.

Weeks earlier, Arturo Macaltao from MOPH told me that I would be called, but it seemed so incredible, I didn't believe it until David called. He explained about their purpose, how they started, and added, "We're located in North Carolina and want to meet you."

"What's the catch?" I didn't ask that question, but that was what ran through my mind. I'd heard about various scams against veterans and assumed they had targeted me.

"We like to help veterans, and we think you're a good candidate for free housing," he said.

"Is that so?"

"You understand recommending you isn't a guarantee, but we'd like to meet with you."

Uh-oh, I thought, here comes the pitch for money, and I

was too irritated to fall for this. "This must be some kind of scam or a joke." I hung up.

Minutes later the phone rang, and it was David Gaines again. "We *are* Operation Coming Home. Check us out on the web." He gave me the link.*

He waited until I checked out their website, and I was highly impressed. This time I listened.

"Before we can take any action," David said, "you'll need to meet with the members of our board."

"Yes, of course," I said and apologized for my skepticism.

He laughed and said not to worry about it. "As I said, you're a candidate, but you need to know that we're also interviewing others."

"Sure, I understand. You can't build a house for every wounded warrior." They owed me nothing, and I was excited just to be considered.

We had two meetings. The first time they wanted to meet me and find out my needs. It was an informal sharing of what they did and how, as a nonprofit charity, their funds came from contributions.

When they asked, I told my story, and they listened intently and asked a few pertinent questions. I enjoyed talking with them.

We got together again a few weeks later "to talk more about your needs in the house." I was overjoyed to know I was still a candidate.

This time we were more relaxed and friendly. After perhaps ten minutes, David said, "We have approved you for a house."

Those words surprised me, but it didn't stop there. They

---

* "Operation Coming Home," Home Builders Association of Raleigh-Wake County, accessed March 15, 2019, http://www.hbawake.com/operation-coming -home.html.

said I would meet with Rich Van Tassel from Royal Oaks. I was so stunned, I'm not sure I took it all in, but they gave me all the details and said, "We're going to build your dream house." Even though I had hoped they would choose us, the announcement surprised me, and I hardly knew what to say except to thank them.

"We're going to build your dream house."

"We're going to build this house for you, and it will be large enough for everything you need. The God that's up there in the skies—" David pointed toward heaven, "knows who'll live in this house. And we want it to be you."

"That's my God you're talking about, so I accept the wonderful gift from Operation Coming Home." As I said those simple words, I hoped they realized how deeply I appreciated what they were doing for Rosemarie and me.

David Gaines told me he didn't know much about the area where they wanted to build us a house, because it was a new neighborhood. When he told me the location, I answered— excitedly, "That's only ten minutes away from our church."

We met, and he showed me the land and the architectural drawings. I looked at them and was grateful.

Although they don't ask or expect us to promote them, since then, I'll never be able to write or say enough good things about that nonprofit organization. We met several people from Operation Coming Home, and before long they became good friends. They truly wanted to help.

And it was an exciting moment for me.

But there was more.

Later that day, Meredith Iler called us from Texas. I remembered her because she had visited me at our apartment in Washington, DC. She had been friendly and I liked her very much.

At the time, she told me that she was with an organization called Helping a Hero—which I knew nothing about, and I didn't ask her about it. She made some mention about building a house for us. I didn't say much, but I didn't believe her. Or maybe I wouldn't allow myself to believe. If I had believed, I would have gotten excited about it, and then if it didn't happen, I'd be thrown back into depression. I thanked her and appreciated her visit.

On the phone after she and I reminisced about her inspiring visit with me in the hospital, she said, "Here's the reason I'm calling you." She went on to remind me that she represented an organization called Helping a Hero. "We build houses for wounded warriors." She said, "And we want to build *you* a house."

"For me?" I sputtered for a few seconds, because I didn't know what to say to her. "Let me—let me call you back."

I turned to Rosemarie and told her about the phone call. "They also want to build a house. For us. Now we have two offers."

"What are we going to do?" Rosemarie asked.

"I've already made a commitment with David Gaines and Operation Homecoming, and I think we should go ahead."

Rosemarie agreed that I needed to honor my commitment.

I called Meredith back, thanked her for her offer, and told her how much I appreciated it—and I truly did. "However, we've made a commitment to Operation Homecoming. You can give the house to someone else who truly needs it."

We had a lengthy conversation and she said, "You are the only one we want to help. Do you suppose we could talk to David Gaines, and our two organizations could do it together?"

"I don't know," I said, "but I can give you the contact information."

That afternoon she called David Gaines.

The following day, David Gaines called me. When the subject of Meredith Iler and Helping a Hero came up, he said, "We've never done this before, but our board had an emergency meeting, and we decided to partner with them. Together, we'll build a house for you and Rosemarie."

I was still in shock to realize that two organizations wanted to build us a handicap-accessible home for free.

When Meredith called again, she said that Helping a Hero was excited about working with Operation Homecoming. "Carlos, we want to be a part of God's purpose in your life by building this home *for you*."

Several times she said, "We want to build you this house where you can be independent, and it can be a happy place for you and Rosemarie and your two daughters."

I thanked her. I liked Meredith and was delighted that the two groups were going to build our house together.

On the day the groundbreaking took place, more than two hundred volunteers participated in the start of building our house. Meredith Iler was there, and I grinned in surprised delight to see Sergeant Jessy Maynard among the guests. People took many, many pictures showing the groundbreaking.

For several days I felt dazed, hardly able to keep up with the wonderful events taking place. So much was happening right then. The work was beginning on our house. "It's really, really happening!" I felt I needed to say and keep saying that until it became a reality.

A dozen times, I thanked God for providing so wonderfully. I thought of the words of Paul, who wrote, "Now to him who is able to do immeasurably more than all we ask or imagine, according to his power that is at work within us . . ." (Ephesians 3:20).

David said dozens of local businesses donated money and material, much of it by the builder, Royal Oaks. By partnering together, they built the house a little larger than the original plans called for. I didn't care about the size. It would be our home.

⌒

I can't say enough wonderful things about the gift of the house. The builders worked hard and quickly, and the house was ready for us to move in on December 2, 2011. Once I saw the finished house, I realized how large it was. Even more, the building was beautiful.

As we went from room to room, I marveled that the entire house was handicap accessible. Rosemarie pointed to the beautiful hardwood floors. We had five bedrooms, three full bathrooms, and even a man cave.

"This location is perfect," Rosemarie said to David and Meredith. "It's close to our church, Capilla Cristo Redentor Assembly of God, and our girls attend a nearby Christian school."

"Perfect," I said. And I probably repeated that word twenty times that day. But that's the way I felt.

Operation Homecoming and Helping a Hero had been so good to us—just giving us the house would have been enough. But then David said, "Before you move in, pick out the furniture you want."

He must have seen the shock on our faces because he added, "The Semper Fi Fund and Helping a Hero have joined together on this. So please get everything you and Rosemarie want for the house." We hadn't expected free furniture on top of that. Rosemarie and I kept praising God, marveling at all the things strangers were doing for us.

We checked out places like Rooms to Go and looked until we found exactly what we wanted. We made pictures to show the two groups what we wanted. They bought everything we asked for and had them delivered.

~

We still had one more big shock. We hadn't thought about or considered any kind of ceremony when we moved in. But David, Meredith, and others had.

We arrived at the house the morning of December 2, 2011—our moving-in day. The ceremonies began with a choral group of marines and the presence of military and civilian dignitaries. Among the special guests were representatives from the First Battalion, Second Marines, Weapons Company, 81 mm Mortar Platoon, the unit I deployed with.

We were still stunned by everything. An even bigger shock was to see my company commander and my first sergeant. Ed Dausk, a retired Marine Corps major, was one of the most enthusiastic in helping us get the house.

Among the many wonderful and touching things they did was to help bring our family members from Puerto Rico to the ceremony.

However, my biggest surprise and the most emotional moment for me that day was to look up and see Brian "Doc" Prendigue, one of the hospital corpsmen who saved my life with nine tourniquets in Afghanistan.*

At the end of the ceremony, Doc came up to me, put keys in my right hand, hugged me, and said, "It's your house now."

I cried—mostly from joy—and the realization that hundreds of individuals gave of themselves in the building and donating of money for furniture and other things. And it still touches me to realize that most of the support came from people I didn't know.

---

* Here is a beautiful short video about the ceremony: "Operation: Coming Home III Welcomes Home Sgt. Evans & Family," YouTube video, 3:15, January 4, 2012, https://www.youtube.com/watch?v=sWcgpx0_ixs.

26

A Dog Named Dino

We had met Ed Dausk at the hospital at a Christmas event in 2010, and afterward he kept in touch with us. More than once he said, "I'd like to do something special for you and Rosemarie." He kept mentioning it, but I never said anything.

I knew Ed meant those words. He's a Vietnam vet and a loyal marine, but most of all to me, a good friend.

Rosemarie wanted to give me a dog for my birthday, so she bought an English bulldog, which is the Marine Corps mascot. Without letting me know, she told Ed about the gift, and he drove to our house from Virginia and helped Rosemarie find exactly the dog she wanted for me.

When Rosemarie brought in the dog, she said, "His name is Major Ed." (That's still his official name, but we refer to him as Dino.)

"I'm going to give you this dog," Rosemarie said, "but I'm not going to take care of it. He will be your dog. You'll watch him, feed him, bathe him, and do whatever needs doing."

Stunned, I stared at that cute little dog and reached out for him. He came into my arms, and I held him.

"That is a really, really special birthday gift," I said.

Rosemarie understood that, because she knew how well I responded to challenges.

Almost immediately, Dino and I bonded. Having that dog was like therapy for me. I couldn't ignore him, and he was always there. He stayed by my side, and I depended on him. Learning to take care of Dino was a great help in lifting my depression. In the mornings, Dino came to my bed and irritated me until I got up. And especially in the early days together, he kept me busy.

> Having that dog was like therapy
> for me. I couldn't ignore him,
> and he was always there.

Dino changed my life because he gave me a renewed sense of responsibility.

Rosemarie

The day after we moved into the new house, one of the first things Carlos wanted was go outside. For him, it was a way to say, "If I can get outside my own house, I can go anywhere."

But he didn't tell me he wanted to explore the area on his own and without having someone help him. A few minutes later, I realized he wasn't around. "Carlos! Carlos!"

He didn't answer. "Carlos, where are you?" I started to panic, and then I realized the dog was also gone. I figured out he had gone for a walk, and I tried to relax, but I wasn't very successful at it.

Carlos

I don't know how to explain my excitement over having a house with no steps. The first morning we were there, I went outside in my wheelchair, and it felt good to be on my own and not needing Rosemarie or someone to help me from the house to the street. Before, I had to ask, "Help me here, help me there."

I opened the door, took my dog, and in my wheelchair, I went outside. For the past eighteen months, I had never gone anywhere alone.

Perhaps twenty minutes later I returned, and Rosemarie ran up to me. I could see she was upset.

"Where were you?" she called. "I couldn't find you!"

"I went out to explore the neighborhood." As I said those words and realized how upset Rosemarie was, I apologized for not telling her. "I wanted to do that on my own, to show myself and you that I could get out there."

As we talked and reminded ourselves of the wonderful experience of the day before, I said, "Now we have to pay it forward. We have to figure out what we can do for other people."

Rosemarie hugged me and I knew she felt the same way. So many had done wonderful things for us. They had believed in me when I couldn't believe in myself. I wanted to do that for others.

As my first step to help others, I started working with Operation Coming Home—which was a natural choice. I did everything I could to raise funds for them and help bring awareness of the organization to the community.

They had built a house for me, which I proudly told everyone about—and I knew other vets who had needs like mine. Operation Coming Home had built only two homes for veterans before us. As of this writing, they have completed and given away eleven more houses—and they aren't slowing down.

Helping Our Military Heroes had provided a van for us that I could drive with my right hand. Being able to drive did wonders for me, and it built up my confidence. That's when I first began to realize I could touch other lives and help them because I could travel to where they were.

From that time on, Rosemarie and I became involved more heavily in the ministry, sharing our story and encouraging others who had been as depressed as I had been.

Rosemarie

At our house, we have a patio and lots of space outside. Carlos started playing outside with the girls. I smiled often when I watched him bond with his daughters in a deeper way—and in ways he couldn't when he had been confined to that apartment.

I particularly smiled when I watched Nairoby at play. In the apartment, she used to play with Carlos's prosthetics because she loved the *Iron Man* movie, which was popular at that time. She often hugged him and said to him, "Papi is Iron Man."

Carlos was my hero!

Adjustments

Carlos

Living for two years in the nation's capital wasn't easy for us, but we grew and learned. The people at Walter Reed helped me to feel like part of a community, and I enjoyed being around other wounded warriors and their families. We were a powerful support to each other.

Yet at the same time, Rosemarie and I were eager to go back to our home—back to Fayetteville, North Carolina.

At Walter Reed, we had everything we needed. The medical team was excellent when I was under their care, and I never want to minimize that. The dedicated staff made sure they did everything they could for us.

"How are you doing today?" they'd ask. But it was more than an informal greeting. They truly wanted to know. They listened.

I might say, "My back hurts a little," or "I'm feeling phantom pains in my right leg." I feel constant, ongoing pain, but most people don't understand that it never completely stops. Even now, as I work on this book, my nonexistent legs and my missing left hand have healed, yet my doctor has said, "As an amputee, you'll likely feel that agony every day." He said, "Some people outgrow it. Maybe you'll be one of them."

The Mayo Clinic used the term *phantom-limb situation,*

which referred to any sensory phenomenon from an absent limb. They stated that at least 80 percent of amputees have phantom pain and feeling in the missing limb sometime in their lives, and some experience it to a degree for the rest of their lives.

For me, it feels as if a hundred ants are biting me as they run up and down my legs. One doctor at Walter Reed told me, "I can prescribe medication that usually helps."

> At least 80 percent of amputees have phantom pain and feeling in the missing limb sometime in their lives.

I didn't want to get hooked on drugs—again—so I refused.

I also have nerve pain, which are my nerves sending a message to the limb that's not there. It's like an electrical shock. But I'm getting used to it. Whenever I become extra tired, the nerve pain hits. Sometimes even when I'm active or doing something and stop, it strikes again.

Because I'm a triple amputee, several doctors warned me that it probably will never go away. It is something I must learn how to live with.

Despite that, I'm grateful to God for keeping me alive and thankful for Rosemarie and our two daughters. For those blessings, I can live with pain.

After eighteen months in Washington, DC, we returned to North Carolina, eager to get on with our lives. We still found it strange to have a wonderful home that fitted our needs. Best of all, we could worship again at our home church.

Nothing is perfect. And one thing we missed was that we no longer had a strong support system as we did in Washington. We had been a tight group because we were all wounded in some form.

Then came the adjustments. A case manager at Walter Reed transferred my records to a VA hospital. The transition experience for me was difficult.

While I was still at Walter Reed I began the transition from active duty to being honorably retired. My case manager sent my information to the VA hospital closest to where we would live. That person contacted a case manager in Fayetteville to make my transition a smooth one.

The first time I visited the VA hospital, I realized it was going to be a far different situation than I had at Water Reed when I was still on active duty. I want to be clear that not all VA hospitals are the same, and not every veteran experiences the disappointing treatment I received.

For example, I went to the VA hospital because the prosthesis on my left leg rubbed and it hurt. Perhaps the warmth and efficiency of Walter Reed had spoiled us, but when I went inside the hospital, even though I had an appointment, I encountered long delays, and it always seemed to involve filling out forms to get treatment.

By the terms of medical discharge, my family was also entitled to benefits. If I wanted a simple thing like shots while we lived in DC, I'd have been in and out in less than half an hour. But the local VA, after half an hour, I'd still be sitting and waiting to be seen by someone.

Once when I went to get new prosthetics, they told me I needed a referral from Walter Reed.

"But it's all in the records, and all you have to do is look at my—"

"I'm sorry, but that's the way we have to do it."

We started the process by filling out forms. It took weeks for the new prosthetics to come through.

Another time I asked a nurse if she could give me a bandage for a sore on my left limb.

"I'm sorry, but I can't give you one."

Puzzled, I asked, "Why not?"

"For that you need to have a script [prescription], which you take to the pharmacy."

I shook my head in disbelief. They stocked bandages right there, and I could see them. Not only did I have to go to the pharmacy, but it was in another building.

Never had we been treated indifferently at Walter Reed, but at that VA hospital I felt as if I had to beg for care. I had given myself unreservedly to serve my country. Now that I was a triple amputee, I felt I had earned the right to be cared for. No one would have argued that fact, but the hospital didn't make it easy for me—or for any of us veterans.

Each time I went, I came away angry because of the indifference, or perhaps it was inefficiency. Whenever I needed help with my prosthetics, the VA hospital system made it extremely difficult. I had to make appointments just to talk with someone; never once did I receive immediate attention. I avoided going there and went only when I couldn't figure out any other way to get care.

During that adjustment, several nonprofit organizations helped us. I once said, "What takes the government six months to get anything done, your nonprofit organization does in a week."

Here's another example. I had to go to the VA to get a new

wheelchair. To start the procedure, I had to make an appointment. Weeks later, they finally notified me that I had an appointment. I went to the hospital, filled out the paperwork, and they fitted me for the right chair.

But they didn't have wheelchairs there and had to order them. That doesn't sound so bad. The problem was that once they put in the order, *ten months* passed before they delivered the wheelchair.

If I had appealed to a nonprofit organization, the longest it would have taken is two months.

The same thing also happened when I needed a new hand cycle. I went to the VA and filled out all the paperwork, and then came the wait. I grew tired of waiting and finally called someone from the Semper Fi Fund. On their website, they say they provide immediate financial assistance and lifetime support to injured members of all branches of the service.

Within *one* month, I had a new hand cycle.

I may be prejudiced because of the excellent care I received at Walter Reed. To me, that hospital offers the best treatment in the world. As a wounded warrior, I not only received the treatment I needed, but it was quick and efficient, and they made me feel they cared.

I had realized that a VA hospital in Fayetteville, North Carolina, wouldn't be the same, but I never once felt that any of the personnel there cared about me as a veteran. As I said, it was a difficult transition. It's been five years since Walter Reed sent my records to the VA. Even now, I feel as if I have to beg for treatment.

The media has gotten hold of this VA abuse, and I don't

want to add anything more to it. My hope—and that of many veterans—is that the service will improve.

Rosemarie is a nurse, and she followed everything done to me at Walter Reed. The first time we went to the VA hospital, she didn't like it. I reminded her that we were in transition, and nothing could be as it had been in Washington.

"Our first goal is to adapt to our situation and overcome it," I said. I had no idea how difficult that would be. I'm still trying to adjust to the indifferent care.

God has done a work of grace in us. I still don't like their attitude, but I finally realized I could do nothing to change the policy or the personnel. And (most of the time) I now accept the situation.

I suffered from post-traumatic stress disorder (PTSD)—something probably all of us wounded warriors struggle with. A doctor at the VA Hospital in North Carolina said, "Someday you'll be over this and not have to deal with it."

"Yes, but right now, I do have to deal with it." Often—not always—when I look at my body with no legs and a missing hand, the memories of that explosion come back to me. Or I feel myself barely alive on the helicopter trip. At times I wake up screaming in pain. There's no "just put it behind you," as if you can choose to leave it behind.

By nature I'm athletic. I was heavily involved in sports in high school and stayed in great shape while in the marines. After my injuries, I told one doctor, "Almost every night I go to sleep and when I wake up I've been dreaming about running. And when I wake up I want to run. And then I remind myself, I can't run. I don't have feet."

Each of us wounded warriors is different, and some of us go through PTSD more deeply than others. I tried not to compare myself with others. In the rehab at Walter Reed, we were all competitive, wanting to walk sooner or use a prosthesis faster. It was good for me to be surrounded by others who lost legs and arms. But I still went through my own post-traumatic stress.

One of the things that finally hit me came while I was praying and crying out to God about what I couldn't do. Then the Holy Spirit spoke—I had to recognize my weaknesses and face them, and only then I could start looking at my strengths.

Simple, but I had focused so much on what I didn't have, that I had gotten my eyes off what I still had *and* forgotten that I was in the Lord's hands. Time helps, but even more, the loving support of Rosemarie, family, and friends helps. I rarely have flashbacks these days, and when I do, they're brief and less stressful.

From my experience, I learned to better understand my strengths and weaknesses. I said to myself, "This is reality; you need to work on self-acceptance so you can live a full and productive life."

Rosemarie

The adjustments weren't easy for Carlos, and consequently, not for me. Each visit to the VA seemed to anger him. So I decided to get involved and see if I could help the situation.

I asked questions of anyone who might help, checked everything I could online. I don't remember where I got the information, but one day I called the Federal Recovery Program and spoke to a coordinator named Amy. That governmental agency wants to make sure wounded veterans receive proper care after retirement. Amy was extremely understanding and helpful. Since then, whenever we have a situation where we need help dealing with the VA, Carlos or I call Amy, and she takes care of it.

She helped Carlos receive new prosthetics and sped up his treatment at the VA facility—still not as good as we hoped for, but she truly helped us maneuver the situation. Amy even set it up so that Carlos as well as the girls and I could go to facilities other than the VA to get treatment and obtain his prosthetic devices. Another thing Amy did for us was arrange for us to go a private doctor.

Other adjustments would follow as we grew in our independence. But by then, I had learned to work with the complicated system.

<hr />

When Carlos was angry and frustrated, he took it out on me—I'm sure he wasn't aware of it. One day I thought, I'm paying for everybody's mistakes. For example, if somebody in the hospital doesn't give him what he wants or makes him wait hours, he comes home and turns all his frustration toward me.

Amy from the Federal Recovery Program has been a tremendous blessing to us. Change isn't easy, and Carlos's transition to the VA certainly wasn't. But God keeps lining us up with the right people who help us in vital, practical ways.

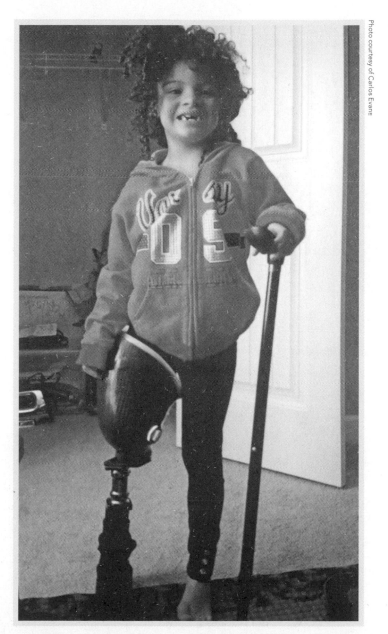

Daughter Nairoby plays with Carlos's prosthetic leg. Washington, DC. 2011.

Navy Corpsman Brian Prendingue and Carlos reunite for the first time since Brian helped save Carlos's life after the explosion. Washington, DC. 2011.

First Lady Michelle Obama, Carlos, and others at the State of the Union Address in Washington, DC. February 12, 2013.

White House photo of the day features Carlos with President Barak Obama. Washington, DC. March 6, 2012.

President Barak Obama and Carlos greet one another at the State of the Union Address in Washington, DC. February 12, 2013.

Rosemarie on foot and Carlos on his hand bike at Camp Humphreys 10K Soldier Run in South Korea. September 2014.

Carlos shows off his medal for riding his hand bike in the Walt Disney World Half Marathon in Orlando, Florida, though finishing the race was his biggest reward. January 8, 2011.

Carlos and Rosemarie in Breckenridge, Colorado, ski for the first time. December 2010.

Carlos preaches at Iglesia Cristiana Manantiales in Santiago, Chile. January 2018.

Carlos prays with the congregation at Casa de Restauracion Emanuel in Barcelona, Spain. 2018.

(L-R) At home with Genesis, Rosemarie, Carlos's dog Starky, Carlos, and Nairoby. December 2017.

Carlos and Rosemarie with coauthor Cecil Murphey. March 2015.

28

Doors Opening Wide

Carlos

Rosemarie wanted to return to Puerto Rico to see our families and our friends. I did too, except I was still afraid to see people from my past. Even though it had been nearly two years since my injuries, I didn't want them to see me as a cripple. But with reservations, I agreed.

In the summer of 2012, we returned to Puerto Rico. As soon as we landed, people rushed forward to greet us. Agustin Montanez, a representative from the governor, was there to greet me. He was a veteran's ombudsman in Puerto Rico.

I hadn't expected that kind of reception, and I was surprised that local media people from the island were on hand to photograph us and interview us.

But most importantly, we were among family and close friends. I felt truly loved by these people who I had known most of my life, and it was an emotional homecoming for me. In Puerto Rico, unlike stateside, people are patriotic, primarily our military people, but I never expected such a crowd, and I didn't know how they were going to react. I needn't have worried. Not only did they give me a warm homecoming, but the mayor of Fajardo, Anibal Melendez, read a proclamation and declared it Sergeant Carlos Evans Day.

I felt overwhelmed to see a lot of people I hadn't seen in two years. This was the first time many of them had seen me with my injuries. Whenever I see someone from my past for the first time after my injury, my mind goes back to when I last saw that person. On this occasion, I kept thinking, the last time I saw you, I had my legs. I assume other amputees go through that as well.

After the homecoming festivities, we attended a luncheon sponsored by Mayor Melendez and our congressman, Pedro Pierluisi. I developed a nice, easygoing relationship with Congressman Pierluisi. In our conversation, he said, "President Obama is coming here. Would you like to meet him?"

"Yeah, why not?"

It was an historic occasion. For the first time in about fifty years, the president was going to visit our country.

I saw the president, shook his hand, and talked with him. It happened quickly, but the president did pause to thank me for my service to our country and, after giving me his characteristic big smile, encouraged me to keep moving forward in my rehabilitation.

In our hometown of Fajardo, I could relax and forget any problems. Being surrounded by the love of our two families made the trip worthwhile. To my surprise, everywhere we went, people treated me like some kind of hero. The news and media widely reported my homecoming.

That trip to Fajardo was one of my most uplifting experiences. I knew I had found my purpose—my calling. Then and even now, I'm still amazed that people want to meet me and hear my story and that of other wounded warriors.

My question to God has now become, "Why are you so good to me?"

While in Fajardo, my friends Kermitt and Annie Otero, who were pastors, asked me to preach in their church, Comunidad Cristiana Restaurando las Naciones.

During our conversation after the service, they encouraged me to meet Raul Feliciano, pastor of Comunidad Cristiana Restaurando las Naciones in New Haven, Connecticut.

Raul had a fine reputation as a great communicator and a compassionate man. Those two qualities didn't always go together. "I'd like to meet him," I said. "I've heard many good things about him."

"And they're all true," Kermitt said. "You'll see when you meet him."

They made plans, and in October of 2012, I visited Raul in Connecticut and spent three days with him. I felt a strong bonding with Raul as well as his wife, Emma. It's hard to describe that bond. Raul understands my heart and my yearning to serve God.

He invited me to preach at Comunidad Cristiana Restaurando las Naciones on January 26, 2013. Pastor Raul invited all four of us, but Rosemarie felt she couldn't take the girls out of their routine, so she drove me to the airport and I flew by myself.

During the flight, I had nothing to do but think. That brought up all my anxieties. "I'm just a little nervous," I thought. "No, I'm scared. What do I have to say? Why would they want to listen to me? I'm not really a preacher. Maybe I will be someday, but I feel empty. Inadequate."

Tears filled my eyes as I cried out to God in desperation. I couldn't think of anything to say to the people.

As I pleaded with God, the Holy Spirit reminded me of the day when I was in the hospital, yelling at God. With my eyes closed, I felt as if I were watching a film about myself. "God, where are you? Where are you, God? Where are you, God, in the middle of all this?"

I felt the Spirit of God speak. "You want to know what I was doing in your life when you were asking where I was? I was with your team in the desert, taking care of them so they could take care of you. I was with your wife, taking care of her so she could take care of you. I was with the doctors, taking care of them so they could take care of you. I was with your best friend, Albert, taking care of him so he could take care of you."

"Forgive me, Lord. You've been in my life all this time. You've been putting people close to me all this time." God *was* with me and had been with me, even in Afghanistan. "Yes, Lord, you've always been there."

Peace came over me. I didn't know what I was going to preach about at the church, but the Lord was with me. That was enough. I would say whatever I felt his Spirit prompting me to say.

My relationship with Raul Feliciano continued after the trip. Four months later, Raul and his wife, Emma, were driving through North Carolina and asked if they could stop at our house and visit. We enthusiastically said yes.

We were overjoyed to see Raul again, and immediately it felt as if we'd been together only a few days earlier. I've rarely felt that close to a person so quickly.

At one point, as we were sitting around talking, he asked me, "What do you plan to do with the rest of your life?"

Because I felt comfortable with him and sensed I could trust him, I tried to be as open as I could. "I feel God has called me to preach—not as a pastor like you, but to spread his message of love around the world."

He smiled and nodded, which encouraged me to add my final statement. "I have no idea how to make that happen."

"Are you talking about engaging in a worldwide ministry?"

"I would like that," I said, "and I'm free to travel, but I don't know how to get started."

"Keep thinking that way," he said. "God can make it possible."

Although I'd thought occasionally about a worldwide ministry, I hadn't voiced the idea before. When I did, Raul understood my heart. He encouraged me to keep talking. And he listened while I continued to tell him some of the marvelous things I had learned in my spiritual life. I emphasized my dependence on the grace of God.

> "I'm preparing to send a team of
> preachers to churches all over Latin
> and South America. . . . I'd like you
> to be on one of those teams."

When I paused, Raul smiled and thanked me. He leaned forward and said, "I'm preparing to send a team of preachers to churches all over Latin and South America—and not just Spanish-speaking churches. As you probably know, many of the congregations are bilingual."

"That's amazing," I said, delighted to know what he was doing.

"I'd like you to be on one of those teams."

"Me?" Even though I wanted to teach worldwide, I still didn't believe in myself. "I . . . I don't know how." Thoughts tumbled through my mind: How could I do that? I'm in a wheelchair. What would I say that people wanted to hear?

For weeks, Rosemarie and I had been praying for guidance on what the Lord wanted me to do. "I want to serve you, Lord," I prayed daily. I felt God speak to me about a number of things, but I had no idea how to make them happen. We had never done any kind of self-promotion—not that I was against it, but it didn't occur to either of us.

"You can share your story and preach the gospel," Raul insisted.

"How can that happen? I'm in a wheelchair, you know."

"You see a wheelchair, but I see a calling. I see a message."

For several minutes, Raul talked about the unlimited ways God can work in life—in *my* life. No one had ever given me more encouragement to speak and share my faith than Raul.

After we talked for several more minutes, Raul leaned back and, almost casually, asked, "Would you be willing to go to Ecuador?"

The question startled me, and I began to think of reasons I couldn't. But then I reminded myself that if God wanted me to go, I could do it.

"Yes."

"In October, the team goes out. I want you to be part of that group."

That was the beginning of my ministry, which has now taken me over large portions of the world.

And I'm not finished yet.

29

Ecuador and Beyond

Going to Ecuador under Raul's sponsorship in October 16, 2013, wasn't just the beginning of my reaching out to the world; it also became a powerful, ministry-shaping time for my wife and me. Rosemarie arranged for friends to care for our daughters, and she went to Ecuador with me. I told my story, but she sat, smiled, and encouraged me.

While we were sitting around talking after my first preaching session, one of the Ecuadorian pastors turned to Rosemarie, "You two should do this together. Let us hear both sides of the story."

"Really? I . . . I've never thought of that," I said.

His words shocked Rosemarie as much as they did me. "I'm not a preacher." Rosemarie pointed to me. "That's what Carlos does."

Although I was regularly preaching at home in other churches, Rosemarie had never said anything in public.

"You can do it," the pastor said.

At first Rosemarie argued against it, insisting, "I'm not a public speaker."

I reminded Rosemarie of how she preached to me when we were kids. Once I thought about it, I knew I wanted her to work with me in the public ministry. "You can do it," I said.

She wasn't so sure, but as we talked, all of us felt the Holy Spirit leading her to tell her side of the story.

"I'm willing to try," she said.

That same day, Rosemarie and I got together and made notes of the important things we had gone through together. "You say this part," I said, "and I'll say this."

The more we reminded ourselves of what we had to share, the more assured both of us became. We did it. And when we spoke—moving back and forth—it was like an explosion. We tried to be as honest as possible and told them all the mistakes we had made and how our marriage almost failed after I became addicted to the painkillers.

Right there—in the middle of the next service—couples stopped listening, turned to each other. They begged each other for forgiveness. Many of them were crying and embracing their spouses. Unlike many people in American church services, they weren't afraid to interrupt us and straighten out their lives.

> All the pain and suffering had been worth it. God has truly turned our lives around so now he can use us to turn other lives around.

"When I heard what happened to you," one pastor's wife told Rosemarie after the service, "I realized how many times I had felt helpless and sorry for myself. But you overcame all those obstacles. Then I felt ashamed. And guilty."

She went on to say, "I was complaining about how terrible everyone was in my life, but you've helped me see that others have gone through worse times. And you handled it."

"And you can too," Rosemarie assured her.

At least a dozen couples had similar stories to tell of bad relationships, pent-up anger, and depression. "Until I heard your story," one husband said, "I didn't realize how good my life was."

Rosemarie and I praised God. All the pain and suffering had been worth it. God has truly turned our lives around so now he can use us to turn other lives around.

Under Raul's auspices, we also went to Cuba, the Dominican Republic, Chile, and several times to Puerto Rico. That's when I realized I really had a ministry and was able to preach and share our testimony.

Raul was right—I was more than a man in a wheelchair; I was a man with a message.

I preached, I taught when asked, and Rosemarie and I conducted several couples' retreats. And it wasn't only overseas; doors began opening for me to speak in schools, prisons, and universities here in the United States. We shared our testimony, and often we visited hospitals, where we spoke with and encouraged other wounded warriors and their spouses.

More and more doors opened, and invitations came to us, but never—not once—did I ever advertise or promote myself. That was God's business. I did only one thing, and that was keep our presence updated on Facebook and depended on the Holy Spirit to impress it on the right people to invite me. (My Facebook account is in both English and Spanish.)

On Facebook I wrote these words: "Let your faith be bigger than your fears." I've illustrated that statement with pictures that show me walking, exercising, and participating in events most people with all four limbs couldn't handle. The photos aren't meant to brag, only to demonstrate the need for courage, an overcoming spirit, and joy. I want to offer hope to those who are experiencing tough times. And I use more than just myself to provide examples; I've also posted photos of my military brothers and sisters, as well as powerful videos showing viewers that the God we serve turns the impossible into the possible.

If you go to Facebook, you can read about (and follow) us by going to "Carlos Evans Toro-Oficial."*

I become excited when I look at photographs and videos of places I've been to spread the good news. As I point out, I've had numerous opportunities to speak in churches, for military groups and organizations, and at big arenas, not just in the United States but also in several countries abroad. Doors opened for me to go to the White House to meet with President Obama and to connect with people like Franklin Graham of Samaritan's Purse and Greta Van Susteren, veteran commentator and television news anchor.

If you check it out, you'll see the many pictures and videos on my page and realize that God has used me—and God can also use anyone willing to obey.†

As more speaking opportunities came our way, Rosemarie

---

* "Carlos Evans Toro—Oficial," Facebook, accessed March 15, 2019, https://www.facebook.com/Carlos-Evans-Toro-Oficial-139263036274812.
† You can also find interviews I've done online. Here are two: "Wounded Soldier to Inspirational Conqueror," YouTube video, 6:45, July 28, 2017, https://youtu.be/GTATisdXbSU; and "Veteran Says He Doesn't Need Feet to Walk with Purpose," YouTube video, 3:37, September 25, 2015, https://youtu.be/msW4wyrDFGk.

and I decided to pay it forward. In September of 2014, we established a nonprofit organization called "Touching Lives Leaving Footprints Foundation, Inc."‡

Both of us wanted to be able to touch other people the same way that we'd been encouraged and helped. A major portion of my public ministry is to speak to other soldiers and their families. Many of them need the kind of boost I received from other wounded warriors.

---

‡ Find us online at http://www.crevans.org.

30

A Man with a Purpose

My most significant issue was to face myself. By nature I'm not very good at looking into my own heart. But I'm learning.

I'm a triple amputee. *Is that how I want to define myself? Is that how I want people to think of me? What am I going to do with the rest of my life? I'm not in the hospital anymore; I'm no longer in the Marine Corps. What happens now? How do I stay active? How can I be fulfilled?*

I thought of my options—and realized I had choices. I said to myself, "I could stay inside my house all day and watch TV." That happens to a lot of wounded warriors who come back home. Like me, they don't have the uniform or the identity they once had. They don't have the jobs and the skills they prized in the military service. Too many have no purpose in staying alive. Without a purpose, their lives feel empty. Meaningless.

Several wounded warriors I'd known well had started drinking heavily. Others went suicidal or turned to drugs. Those situations happen all too often.

For days I asked myself questions, trying to find a new balance for my life. *If I'm no longer in the Marine Corps, who am I? What do I do now?*

Finally I said to myself, "Carlos, you'll never walk on your own legs again. But you're alive. You have a wife and two children. You have a steady paycheck—your pension—that you earned. Besides that, you have a house with no payments. God spared your life in Afghanistan. Why would he have spared your life if he had no purpose for you? How do you show appreciation for the gift of life?"

During that time, I tried to focus on ministry. God has enabled me to talk freely to people, to preach, and share the good news of life in Jesus Christ. But where did I fit in? How was God going to use me?

I started by finding purpose right within my own church, Capilla Cristo Redentor Assembly of God. I went to Pastor Francisco Soltren, and he put me to work. I started working with the youth. Sammy Cruz was then the youth pastor, and he invited me to tell my story to the teens in his church.

I had no idea where the Lord was taking me. And yet never before had I felt so single-minded. I had to have part of my body taken from me before I was ready to give myself totally to God.

Within a short time, Pastor Francisco invited me preach about once a month, and I loved it. That was the beginning. People in our church who heard our story told their friends, and their friends told others. The word spread. Because I was a wounded vet, schools invited me to speak to their students.

After that, I realized that sharing my story and preaching God's purpose had a powerful effect on people. God was using my story and my gift to speak to touch others.

Both Rosemarie and I taught in their vacation Bible school. I also went to other places, such as Fayetteville Technical Community College, Fielding University in Chicago, and nonprofit organizations.

People found me on Facebook, which was and remains the only way we promote our ministry.

Before long, my primary function in our church was to coordinate mission trips for church members, working with budgets and travel.

I'm grateful for our pastor, Francisco Soltren, because I had no idea where the Lord was taking me. And yet I'd never had such a strong sense of purpose in my life to speak whenever doors opened for me.

Because our pastor readily accepted me and put me to work, I felt useful. *I had a purpose.* God could use me. That's when I came up with a statement about myself: Now that I have one hand, I'm touching more people than when I had two hands. I don't have feet, but I'm leaving more footprints than when I had feet.

I became a new man. Or perhaps I started becoming the man God wanted Carlos Evans to become. Now I could give my time—all my time—as well as my mind and heart to serve the Lord.

I stand as an example of someone who has been healed—not with legs restored, but healed inside and made stronger.

God uses our lives to show people who *he* is. I believe strongly that our lives can inspire faith for someone else's miracle.

Here's an example. One day I attended a revival where my friend Jose L. Hernandez was preaching. Right in the middle of his message, Jose stopped to pray for one man. I was next to the man and praying too.

Right in front of me, I saw the miracle take place. Before

Jose prayed, one of the man's arms was noticeably shorter than the other. As Jose prayed, the arm grew instantly until both of them were the same length. As incredible as that sounds, I can only say I saw it happen.

Everyone began to rejoice and praise the Lord. I kept thanking God for the miracle I had just witnessed. Then the Holy Spirit spoke to my heart and reminded me that *my* life is a miracle.

Immediately I thought, Maybe God would do the same for me. And I prayed for it to happen. Then I realized that was not God's plan for me. I didn't need two legs and a hand to be a witness for him.

I should be dead because of my injuries, but God had a destiny for me, and I lived. I could have become a victim of bad experiences, felt sorry for myself, and hated life. But God changed all that. Instead of being a victim, I became a victor.

Every day I celebrate the miracle of life—my life. I'm with the three people I love most. And I have opportunities to share the love of Jesus.

Sometimes I think of the day my boss, Gunnery Sergeant Baez, told me they had kept the flak jacket and helmet I wore the day I was blown up. A flak jacket is a sleeveless jacket, like a vest, made of heavy fabric reinforced with Kevlar and worn as protection against bullets and shrapnel. Many people don't realize that Kevlar is made from a special kind of plastic and is strong enough to stop bullets and knives. It's often described as being five times stronger than steel of the same weight.

"I saved it and wondered if you'd like to have it," Baez said.

"No! I don't want it! It reminds me of too many horrible things."

We talked, and finally I said, "All right. Let's go pick it up." I got it, saw it, and too many painful memories filled my heart and mind. I picked up the vest and my helmet and took them home in a military packing case. I never wanted to see the flak jacket again. I told my wife to put the case in the closet. I didn't want to see it.

One Sunday I was going to preach at my church. It was the Fourth of July weekend in 2013. As I prayed and prepared, I felt in my heart that the Lord wanted me to pick up the jacket. I asked Rosemarie to get out the case. She knew I needed to look at it on my own, so she left while I did.

My helmet was all beat up and smashed, and it was no longer possible to wear it. I assumed it had been blown off my head and was beaten out of shape by the shrapnel. I could barely turn my eyes to my jacket, which was covered with my blood.

> Sometimes what we think is a
> failure in our lives could be a
> stepping stone toward victory.

Rosemarie cleaned it, I helped a little bit, and I took it to church. I started preaching and I put my flak jacket on. The theme of my message was that sometimes what we think is a failure in our lives could be a stepping stone toward victory. It could be the strongest weapon in our lives.

Today, when I see that flak jacket, I don't look at it as a failure. I see it as a victory.

One of the last things I said in my sermon that day was, "The day of my accident was the worst day of my life. Today is the best day of my life because God has helped me conquer my fear, and I'm enjoying my life to the fullest."

People sometimes ask what I say to people who focus on the terrible things that happened to me. I tell them, "Yes, bad things happened, and I wish I weren't a triple amputee. But those experiences have made me a happier, stronger person. I don't think I'd have the deep relationship with the Lord that I have today if it hadn't been for Afghanistan."

I think of the words of Job, who said that he first knew of God by what he heard, but now he had seen him with his own eyes. That's how I feel.

My view of life is clearer and my way is more open than ever before. I'm also a better husband and father for having gone through that experience. I don't feel incomplete because I'm missing both legs and a hand. I feel complete because I'm part of the body of Christ. I'm exactly the way God wants me to be.

God has also given me a speaking and teaching platform, and I can do things I never dreamed of doing before. The Word of God is filling my life, and I'm living my life much better than before. That's why I don't have any regrets.

Rosemarie

A lot of people still come to me personally and say, "I know this is very hard," "I'm sorry this happened," or in some way try to offer me sympathy.

At first I used to thank them and appreciate them for being

sensitive to our situation. But Carlos and I have grown spiritually since then. When Carlos first came home, both of us had a victim mentality. But now that's gone.

Although I rarely respond when people start telling me how sad they are for me and how terrible my life must be, I really want to say, "Don't be sorry for me, because I don't need pity and sympathy. We are living our lives now, and they're full. We're both doing things we've never done before."

Not long ago I was reading the story of Joseph and his brothers to my daughters. After Joseph saved the brothers' lives by storing food in Egypt, they said how sorry they were for what they had done to him. They focused on what they had done wrong and were afraid he would punish them.

But Joseph focused on what God had done and said, "Don't be afraid. Am I in the place of God? You intended to harm me, but God intended it for good to accomplish what is now being done. . . . So then, don't be afraid" (Genesis 50:19–21).

People look at Carlos and feel sorry for him. Yes, I wish Carlos had his own legs and a hand, but God has made our lives so wonderful since the injury. God turned everything bad into good.

In no way could our lives have been so fulfilled if we hadn't been through all the pain and hardship. I can tell you without hesitating, it was worth it.

31

Traveling the World

Carlos

Liliana and Enrique Rivera, an army couple in our church in Fayetteville, received orders to South Korea. Once they were there and established with a church, they spoke to the pastors about me and the possibility of having me come to South Korea to speak. They also contacted the command sergeant, Major Sotorosado, about me.

Sergeant Major Estevan Sotorosado, the senior enlisted adviser of the Second Combat Aviation Brigade, was also stationed in South Korea. He conferred with his pastor there to see if they could invite Rosemarie and me to speak at the church, and they agreed.

Then he spoke to the chaplains at Camp Humphreys—an army garrison and also home to Desiderio Army Airfield, the busiest US Army airfield in Asia. In addition to the airfield, there are several US Army direct support, transportation, and tactical units located there, including the Second Infantry Division's Second Combat Aviation Brigade.

"What do you think I should do?" I asked my pastor. I also asked a few other close friends.

Without exception, each of them said, "Go for it. Do it."

Rosemarie and I said yes. We got on a plane from Fayetteville to Chicago. From there it was a direct flight to South

Korea. After a journey of nearly seven thousand miles, we arrived on Saturday, September 27, 2014.

Enrique and Liliana picked up Rosemarie and me at the airport and drove us to the base. I felt like a celebrity and personally met the leaders who had extended the invitation.

My coming at was in conjunction with Suicide Awareness Month—a time when chaplains speak to soldiers, marines, airmen, and sailors to promote awareness and help military personnel to avoid committing suicide.

Between the church and the chaplains, everyone worked together, paid all our expenses, and made arrangements for Rosemarie and me to be in South Korea for a week. I was able to speak to the soldiers of the Second Combat Aviation Brigade on Saturday and Sunday, September 27 and 28, 2014, and during the week.

≈

Sergeant Major Estevan Sotorosado explained that it was important for me to come—a true wounded warrior who had faced the worst. He pointed me out as a living example that no matter how bad the soldiers might think they have it, they could endure, move, and take on any challenge in life.

Then I spoke. "Life is a challenge and full of obstacles," I said to those who had gathered to listen to me. It was a free day at the base, and yet soldiers filled the room. "You'll always have things in your life that will push you to go that extra mile."

After speaking a few minutes, I added, "What looks like an obstacle provides a stepping stone for your goals—for whatever you want to do in your life."

I truly meant those words—and I'd learned them the hard

way. As I told them my story and poured out my heart, I sensed they were with me.

"I want to tell you three things in my life that make me happy—that bring a smile to my face when I wake up every morning. The first is friends, the second is family, and the third is faith. They are the foundations in my life that make me the person I am today and the person I want to be tomorrow."

I finished by speaking openly about my faith in Jesus Christ and what he had done for me. "Sometimes in life, you'll need someone to stop the bleeding so you can achieve any goal you've set. It could be your battle buddy, your roommate, a family member, a friend back home pushing you forward, never allowing you to quit. I had all that, because of my faith in Jesus Christ."

When I stopped speaking, spontaneous clapping broke out, and it seemed to go on for a long time.

That was a beautiful experience for us. More than once I stopped, closed my eyes, and said, "God, you are totally awesome. Only you could do all these things."

That afternoon, Sergeant Sotorosado presented me with a special brigade coin and thanked me for visiting a Wounded Warrior Unity Ride. Colonel William D. Taylor, commander of Second CAB, formally handed me a jersey of the Second CAB, Second Infantry Division.

⌐

That weekend I entered a ten-kilometer race along with hundreds of soldiers, and I was the only one with a hand cycle. Some of them came on bikes, but most of them ran.

I didn't have my prosthetic legs right then, and they could

see me without my legs, although I did wear my prosthetic hand so I could use the hand cycle. I felt it was good to let the military personnel see me without my limbs.

As one soldier said to me, "Seeing you with your missing hand and legs, I don't have an excuse. If Carlos can do it, I can do it."

For me to know that I had been a source of encouragement more than made the trip invaluable to me.

From that experience, I learned that leaders can speak all they want, but if they're not in touch with the people under them or around them, they won't open up. Going through that 10K race and allowing others to see the real me seemed to open those runners up to me. As they watched me, I believe they truly saw me as one of them.

> Going through that 10K race and
> allowing others to see the real me seemed
> to open those runners up to me.

The next day Rosemarie and I both preached at the church. It was very touching to see how the community needed a lot of spiritual awakening in their lives, especially married couples. Rosemarie and I spent the rest of the week ministering to military couples and families.

That was a beautiful experience for us. It was the fulfillment of God working in our lives. I was reminded of that by every word of encouragement I got from someone.

God, you led me here. You opened this door and all the others. I would never, never have dreamed that I would have traveled around the world like this. Thank you for making it happen. Thank you for using Rosemarie and me.

32

Polar Plunge

In 2015, Rosemarie and I visited the Billy Graham Library at the Cove, near Charlotte, North Carolina. While there, Rosemarie saw a piece of literature about a weeklong marriage retreat in Alaska. It was a free event for wounded warriors.

As soon as we returned home, Rosemarie went online and applied. A few months later, we received a telephone call, and the person asked if we still wanted to go.

"Yes, we do," Rosemarie said.

We were accepted as one of nine couples invited by Samaritan's Purse, which sponsored Operation Heal Our Patriots for their July marriage retreat at Lake Clark near Anchorage, Alaska.

All the men were wounded warriors, and as I learned, I wasn't the only amputee, though I was the worst injured. We had all struggled with PTSD, TBI, or some kind of severe injury.

The moment we got out of the airplane, we saw a small community of people waiting for us. And what I saw on this trip was a manifestation of God's love through the people who were surrounding us. They provided cabins for each couple. Everything was handicap accessible. We went kayaking—my first time—on a lake there in Alaska. And we went fishing every day; on the first day, Rosemarie caught a twenty-seven-inch lake trout and, from what they called an action track-chair, I caught several Arctic grayling.

We did different kinds of activities that allowed Rosemarie and I to connect because we were able to focus on each other. Our daughters were with Rosemarie's parents, and this was time alone, just us.

Samaritan's Purse provided wilderness experiences for us—the first such encounters for Rosemarie and me—but the focus of the retreat was on each other, and our classes were all Bible-based marriage enrichment classes. As one woman said, "It's a place to heal and not worry about anything at home. Couples can connect and reconnect with each other."

Rosemarie and I had always thought our marriage was strong and we got along well. But once we were there, teachings of the chaplains really opened our eyes that there were things we needed to work on together and individually. Those wonderful lessons helped strengthen our marriage.

One of them was discovering how different Rosemarie and I are. The insights helped us to accept each other's differences and love each other for who we are. And the lessons went beyond just our relationship; they also helped us understand our children—why they acted as they did—and gave us tools for becoming better parents. For example, I had to learn to be more patient—something Rosemarie had tried to get through to me.

As Chaplains Jim Fisher and his wife, Lori, as well as Dan Stephens and his wife, Linda, spoke warmly to all of us, I absorbed their words. It seemed as if everything they said applied directly to me. God used these people as his special messengers to give me a blessing.

Franklin Graham, the head of Samaritan's Purse, was there with his wife, Jane. We got acquainted with both of them and enjoyed our time with them. I especially liked it when he talked about being a motorcycle rider, and about some of the things he did in ministry.

Greta Van Susteren, then host of the Fox News program *On the Record*, was there with her husband, John Coale.

All week long we were challenged to do the polar plunge.

"Hey, are you going to do the polar plunge? Are you going to jump? Are you going to do it? Are you?"

"I don't think so," was my answer. But later I changed my mind. "Why not?" I asked myself. I knew how to swim, and if others could take the plunge, I could too.

> The polar plunge symbolized
> being at a place with no worries
> and a lot of freedom.

Before we went to the dock, I spoke with Franklin, who was wearing sneakers and not dressed for the plunge. I kidded him, and when he said he wasn't taking the plunge, I said, "Come on, why not take the plunge with us? I'm going to do it. Look, I'm a triple amputee and I'm going to get in the water. If I can do it, you can do it."

He laughed and said, "Okay, I'll join you." Then he said, "Why don't you ask Greta to jump too?" So when we got to the dock, I asked her. At first she was a little reluctant, but finally she said she would.

Once we were all assembled, Franklin turned to me. "You
lead us."

I was the first to take the plunge—which is typical of me. I
like to get it done and over with. While I was in the freezing
water, I also felt free—as if I had legs and was totally unlimited. To me, the polar plunge symbolized being at a place
with no worries and a lot of freedom.

I swam to the dock and someone wrapped a heavy towel
around me.

"How was it?" they asked.

"Cold. So cold I can't feel my feet."

Everyone laughed, and I think some of them relaxed.

Franklin followed me, and someone pushed Greta into
the frigid waters. After she got out of the water, she didn't
complain, and she even smiled—as soon as she stopped
shivering.*

After that, just about everyone leaped off the dock. And
it wasn't just us husbands who jumped into the water. Most
of the wives timidly took the plunge. Rosemarie was one of
those who jumped in.

I was so excited that I jumped in a second time, right behind
her. After I got out of the water, I couldn't wipe the grin from
my face as I saw the excitement in Rosemarie because she was
having so much fun. She deserved it—and more.

━━━

Before we went home, I was interviewed about the Alaska marriage retreat. "When Christ is the center of your relationship

---

* "How a Triple Amputee Marine Vet Got a Fox News Host to Plunge into Ice Water," PopularMilitary.com, September 30, 2015, http://popularmilitary.com/how
 -a-triple-amputee-marine-vet-got-a-fox-news-host-to-plunge-into-ice-water.

you can go through hard times," I said. "I can assure you that if Christ is the center of your relationship he'll give you the strength to go through the ups and downs and to love each other. The reason we say that is because we've lived it."

I added, "I know in my heart that I'm going to be a better husband. I'm going to be a better father. I'm going to be a better man of God."†

One of the last events at the marriage retreat was a memorable ceremony along the shores of Hardenberg Bay. There we committed ourselves afresh to God and to our spouse. The big moment for me was when each of us turned to our spouse and said, "Please forgive my past actions." We also promised to offer each other grace in our future failures.

And finally, we resolved to build our lives on a firm foundation of Jesus Christ and his Word.

---

† "A Celebration of Marriage and Freedom," Samaritan's Purse, July 4, 2015, https://www.samaritanspurse.org/article/a-celebration-of-marriage-and-freedom.

33

Celebration in Fayetteville

The Lord put it on our hearts to do something to reach the community where we live—our hometown of Fayetteville, North Carolina. After talking it over with Rosemarie and her father, we decided to rent the Crown Arena in Fayetteville for twenty thousand dollars—money we didn't have, but we felt God was leading us and would provide. From the beginning, we decided that everything would be bilingual—English and Spanish.

We started by arranging a free breakfast and invited all pastors of the Hispanic churches in the community. I also invited various parachurch ministries. That's the first time that had ever been done. And they came. We told them what we had in mind and that we wanted to reach our community for Christ. Among the special invitations to worship, I asked Jose Luis Reyes, Samuel Hernandez, and Alex Zurdo. We really promoted the event.

The pastors agreed to support the event that I called Celebration. The purpose was to celebrate life. I didn't ask for any money, only for prayers and volunteers at the event. It took us almost a year to make it happen.

A month before the planning, we had incorporated as CR Evans Ministries. We didn't ask for money, but we shared our vision. And to our delight, generous contributions came in and paid for the arena. I started this idea in October 2014, and we needed almost a year to get it done. We held Celebration on Wednesday, September 26, 2015.

We made a video in Spanish with English subtitles to show people that I, a triple amputee, was enjoying life to the fullest. It shows me in many scenarios—in our house, sky diving, bicycling, fishing, kayaking, and even with President Obama.*

We had prayed for a good crowd, and even though it rained that day, to our surprise, almost five thousand people came.

We wanted to reach our Spanish-speaking community as well as our military community. Both communities came and sang songs of praise, and it seemed as if the applause would never stop. Rosemarie and I preached that evening and called for people to turn to Jesus Christ as their Savior. More than five hundred people came forward.

The pastors of the different churches involved worked together, and we turned the names of those who made decisions over to the churches near them. Our messages focused on one theme: Look at yourself through the mirror of the cross.

Even now, we still receive testimonies of growing congregations where the pastors are discipling those new believers. We were especially touched when we learned that our neighbors surrendered their lives to the Lord.

At first it was difficult for me to go places, talk to church leaders, and tell them what we were doing. I felt inadequate, as if they were asking, "Who are you?" But by God's grace I did it. And after a time it became easier and more natural as my confidence built.

---

* "Celebracion 2015," YouTube video, 7:08, September 26, 2015, https://www.youtube.com/watch?v=wcPAV5m72Wc.

One of the things I realized was that God will use any of us who give ourselves. All we have do is say (and mean), "Lord, use me. Here I am." And God will use us by opening doors and giving us the opportunities.

To follow my goals—my dreams—I didn't need feet. I needed only faith.

I also learned that when God puts something on our hearts—even if we don't have the resources—if we believe, God will provide the resources as well as the opportunities.

To follow my goals—my dreams—I didn't need feet. I needed only faith. In the beginning, I was so worried about being able to stand that I didn't realize that during my whole journey, I had been surrounded by a village of people, lifting me up and walking together in this pathway of faith.

Even when I was in the hospital or at home in my wheelchair, I reminded myself that I was always standing on the foundation of family, love, hope, and grace. Yes, I had problems, setbacks, and discouragements, but I was still able to stand firm in my faith that, as an old song says, every day with him is better than the day before.

I believe that.

I live that.

One experience wasn't a world trip, but it meant so much to me. On November 14, 2016, a reporter from CBN's *700 Club* came to my house and interviewed me.

"If you could go back to the Carlos who was at Walter Reed in the hospital bed," Jonathan Scott asked, "what would you want to tell him?"

The question shocked me because no one had ever asked me before. "I would tell that Carlos in the hospital bed, who just arrived at the Bethesda Naval Hospital, 'Starting today, you need to learn to have patience because from now on you're about to live the best days of your life.'"

And it was true. When I was there, I thought I was going to die. At other times, I wanted to die. Because of God's grace, however, I've been living the best days of my life—since my injury.

I went back to Germany in April of 2016, with many from the Semper Fi Fund and other wounded vets—marines, airmen, sailors, and soldiers. We went to Ramstein Air Base and Landstuhl Regional Medical Center, where they took care of me after I left Afghanistan.

We appeared before the staff of nurses. Of course, most of them were not serving there in 2010, but there were a few, and they told me their impressions of when I came into Landstuhl.

I had been in such pain then, I don't remember anything. Those few nurses and staff members who remembered me told me how they reacted. Tears filled the eyes of several of them, and as I listened, I felt a powerful emotional connection.

It was as if they had opened a chapter I hadn't read in the book of my life. I cried a few tears, but most of the time I was filled with deep joy. Several times I reached out to touch them with my right hand and thank them.

The leader of our group said, "We want you to see the job you've done and how what you do for our wounded warriors is worth it. These men are here today because you helped to save their lives."

He pointed out, as all of us well knew, that we were brought in, severely wounded, often unconscious, and sick. Now we were living proof that their commitment and skills had paid off.

"These men are here to say thank you. Each one of them came directly here from Iraq or Afghanistan."

The hospital had the records, so I could see the room where I stayed on May 22. I also got to experience a simulation flight inside a C-130C, which was like the plane that brought me to Germany. I stared at the American flag right in front of me, and I listened to the noise of the plane. I turned to Rosemarie and said, "I know I'm not supposed to remember any of this, but this moment, I'm looking at the flag and hearing the sounds of the airplane, and I feel a very strong connection. I kind of remember this."

I started crying. I cried a lot on that trip, as did many others. We were so happy to be alive. While there, I realized how many skilled and caring people had made that possible. They cared and did their best. And because of that, I'm alive today.

My most powerful experience, though I didn't remember it from my time right after my injury, was learning that the hospital was sending families of wounded from Germany to the United States. They did everything—and treated our families as kindly and carefully as they must have treated us.

After my visit to Landstuhl, I realized that even in the most critical and life-threatening time in my life, I had never been alone. God was standing by my side, and God was using his human angels to minister to me.

34

Summing Up

The one thing I'd like readers of this book to do is commit themselves to stand beside those who are in need. As I learned through my experience with other wounded warriors, there are many who feel untouched and unloved.

My appeal is not just to stand by wounded warriors, but to reach out in any way you can to needy, hurting people. I'm still paying it forward in gratitude to those who reached out to me—especially at the times when I felt cast off and alone.

I've been blessed by being invited to speak all over the world and I'm amazed that God uses me. On August 4, 2016, I went to the Lincoln Memorial because I had been invited to preach by Luis Nevarez at a prayer rally for our nation. I stood right where Martin Luther King gave his "I Have a Dream" speech. I felt as if I were on holy ground. I stared at the people and felt awe just at being there.

As I prepared to speak, a thought struck me. "Six years ago, I flew in here through this place. I flew in sick, in a coma. I couldn't do anything for myself. Now here I am, all this time later, preaching the gospel here."

That is the power of God. That is God's grace in action. And that is an experience I took home with me. The things God can do aren't limited.

In 2010, I couldn't believe that God would take me—a physically and emotionally broken man—and use his life to give hope to others. To encourage them to say, "With God, nothing is impossible." Or as Jesus put it, "Everything is possible for one who believes" (Mark 9:23).

As Rosemarie and I were going through those first three years after the injury, we learned so much about each other, but mostly we grew in our love and commitment to God.

Neither of us had any idea that the day would come when we would use our experience to speak to and counsel other couples in pain.

Several times we had to return to the foundation of our relationship—back to the day we got married. We married because we loved each other. And through all the stages of our lives, we still love each other—and we love each other more.

> **Standing has nothing to do with having feet. Standing is being in God's will.**

Because we've been through so much together and have grown from this experience, we are able to touch other people. God is love, and he reminds me that we can stand firm on his promises.

I have learned that standing has nothing to do with having feet. Standing is being in God's will. Standing is waking up every day and knowing that I'm doing my best to be in God's purpose in my life. And going to sleep knowing that I'm trying to fulfill God's purpose in my life.

So today when I talk about walking, with or without using prosthetics, I'm standing. I'm standing in my relationship, I'm standing in my marriage, I'm standing to my family, to my daughters, to my kids, to my ministry.

Before I had two hands—and did a lot of things—but with one hand, I'm doing more things. Touching more people. I'm leaving a bigger mark, because I'm doing it with my heart.

When you do something with your heart, and do it in God's will, following God's purpose, whatever looks impossible, it's possible.

APPENDIX

A Few Facts About Marriages of Wounded Warriors

- An estimated two out of three marriages fail for troops suffering from combat trauma (http://ptsdusa.org). (Some sources say three out of four marriages fail.)
- In the United States, nearly two million people live with limb loss. Each day more than five hundred Americans lose a limb (https://www.amputee-coalition.org).
- April is Limb Loss Awareness Month.
- As of the 2014 fiscal year, 3.9 million veterans receive disability compensation (http://www.va.gov/vetdata/Vet eran_Population.asp).
- An estimated 48.9 million noninstitutionalized civilians in the United States have a disability. Almost half of them (about 24 million) are considered to have a severe disability. Almost one in five Americans has a disability (http://www.infouse.com/disabilitydata/disability/1_1 .php).
- Fifty-two million caregivers provide care for adults with a disability or illness (https://www.caregiver.org/care giver/jsp/content_node.jsp?nodeid=439).
- November is National Family Caregiver Month.

Veterans with chronic PTSD showed
- More numerous and severe relationship problems
- Poorer family adjustment
- Higher divorce rates
- Less self-disclosure and emotional expression
- Greater anxiety related to intimacy[*]

Men with PTSD and veterans who were physically aggressive with their wives[†] scored higher on
- Major depression
- Drug abuse or dependence
- War-zone atrocity exposure

Wives commonly complained of
- Stress of multiple deployments
- Husband's changed personality
- Caregiver and spouse conflicts
- Military-to-civilian transition
    - Financial hardship/disability determination
    - Anger
- Chronic stress
- Loss of intimacy
- Violence and abuse
- Compassion fatigue

---

[*] Candace M. Monson, Casey T. Taft, and Steffany J. Fredman, "Military-Related PTSD and Intimate Relationships: From Description to Theory-Driven Research and Intervention Development," *Clinical Psychology Review* 29, no. 8 (December 2009): 707–14.

[†] Casey T. Taft et al., "Posttraumatic Stress Disorder, Anger, and Partner Abuse Among Vietnam Combat Veterans," *Journal of Family Psychology* 21, no. 2 (June 2007): 270–77.

Acknowledgments

We want to thank our parents, Frank, Millie, Rafael, and Virginia, for their unconditional support and love. Our daughters, brothers, sisters, and extended family for standing together with us. Also, our church family, Capilla Cristo Redentor, and other churches around the world that keep us in their prayers.

Our journey of pain and victories have been surrounded by many people and organizations that touched our lives at some point. We wouldn't be able to enjoy life today without the seed of hope that was planted by each one of you. Thank God for the strength that you provided.

We want to thank the medical staff and volunteers at Landstuhl Regional Medical Center and Walter Reed Bethesda Medical Hospital for their expertise and caring support.

Along with these, we acknowledge the 2010–2012 wounded warrior class and families. Thanks for celebrating our victories, crying with us in our darkest moments, and lifting us up when we were ready to surrender. Only those who walk this path can really understand the struggles and help create ways to succeed and enjoy life as it is. Thanks for the advice, tricks, and stories that led us to understand our new life and challenges.

A special thanks to all the amazing people and organizations that have been present in this process, especially Gunnery Sergeant Albert Andino; Joel Evans; Major Ed Dausk,

First Battalion, Second Marines, Weapons Company, 81 mm Mortar Platoon; Heather Bernard; Jordan Hall; and Janine Canty.

We are grateful for the support and encouragement from Semper Fi Funds, Operation Homefront, Help Our Military Heroes Charity, Operation Coming Home, Helping a Hero, Yellow Ribbon Fund, Operation Second Chance, Veteran Airlift, Disabled Sports USA, Achilles International, Military Order of the Purple Heart, Disabled Veterans of America, American Red Cross, United Service Organizations (USO), Samaritan Purse's Operation, and Heal Our Patriots.

Special thanks to our coauthor, Cecil Murphey. Cec spent many, many hours with us, probing for details. His experience as an interviewer and professional writer have brought our story to life. We also are indebted to our agents, Deidre Knight and Elaine Spencer of The Knight Agency. Thanks for your patience, encouragement, and understanding. We're grateful that you helped us relive our life experiences and continue the healing process through this book and your friendship.